Fiscal Fitness

for School Administrators

Fiscal Fitness

for School Administrators

How to Stretch Resources and Do Even More With Less

Robert D. Ramsey

CORWIN PRESS, INC.
A Sage Publications Company
Thousand Oaks, California

For information:

Corwin Press, Inc.
A Sage Publications Company
2455 Teller Road
Thousand Oaks, California 91320
E-mail: order@corwinpress.com

Sage Publications Ltd.
6 Bonhill Street
London EC2A 4PU
United Kingdom

Sage Publications India Pvt. Ltd.
M-32 Market
Greater Kailash I
New Delhi 110 048 India

Printed in the United States of America

Library of Congress Cataloging-in-Publication Data

Ramsey, Robert D.
    Fiscal fitness for school administrators: How to stretch resources
& do even more with less / by Robert D. Ramsey.
        p. cm.
    Includes bibliographical references (p. 179).
    ISBN 0-7619-7607-8 (cloth: acid free paper)
    ISBN 0-7619-7608-6 (pbk.: acid free paper)
        1. Education—United States—Finance—Handbooks, manuals, etc.
2. School management and organization—United States—Handbooks,
manuals, etc. I. Title.
    LB2825 .R35 2000
    371.2'06'0973—dc21   00-009509

This book is printed on acid-free paper.

01   02   03   04   05   06   07   10   9   8   7   6   5   4   3   2   1

Production Editor: Denise Santoyo
Editorial Assistant: Candice Crosetti
Typesetter: Rebecca Evans

Table of Contents

Preface

Why This Book Is Different

It's happening everywhere. Schools are being called on to stretch existing resources and to do even more with less. Expectations are escalating, while resources are often dwindling.

Many federal dollars for education have dried up. What money remains is frequently wrapped in red tape. At the same time, many state legislatures can't decide how they want to finance public schools, and local taxpayers just want relief. All across the country, many school budgets are flat, falling behind, or taking a nose dive. Principals are caught in the middle.

Unfortunately, they don't teach school administrators about creative resource management, budget cutting, and cost containment in graduate school. Likewise, resource stretching and belt-tightening don't come with an instructional manual. Until now!

Fiscal Fitness for School Administrators is the first-ever comprehensive guide for making the most of all school resources and surviving, even thriving, in hard times. This no-nonsense handbook covers every aspect of fiscal fitness for today's schools, from how to cut costs without cutting essential programs and how to accomplish as much or more with less staff to how to run a low-cost, no-frills activity program and how to find, raise, and attract money for your school.

Based on years of frontline experience, the guide also spells out school-tested ways to stretch curriculum dollars, get better administration for less money and build business partnerships that really pay off. Other sections include

- A Step-by-Step Budget Reduction Process That Really Works
- How to Run an Effective Staff Development Program on a Shoestring

- How to Save Money on Public Relations and Still Get the Job Done
- How to Get the Community to Shoulder More of the Responsibility
- How to Get Students to Help You Do More With Less
- How to Do More in Less Time

This information can't be found anywhere else. And best of all, each chapter of this one-of-a-kind sourcebook is packed with real-world examples, guidelines, checklists, procedures, and ready-to-use forms that can be adopted or adapted in any school regardless of size. There isn't a principal anywhere who doesn't have questions about how to make the most of what he or she has and how to do even more with less. This unique guide has answers that no other book offers.

As it turns out, austerity isn't the end of the world after all. It can be a needed wake-up call to help administrators energize staffs and clarify priorities. It is possible to make fiscal fitness work to the advantage of students and the entire community. *Fiscal Fitness for School Administrators* can show you how to make it happen.

Acknowledgments

More people than I can count or even remember have influenced the creation of this book. These few I must acknowledge for their special contributions: Nancy Spannaus and Tom Stringer for the gift of the title and much of the wisdom and ideas contained in the text; Robb Clouse and all the other people at Corwin Press who supported and nurtured the book to fruition; and my wife, Joyce, who once again transformed hieroglyphics into a first-class manuscript. This book would not have happened without them.

Robert D. Ramsey, Ed.D.

About the Author

Robert D. Ramsey is a lifelong educator who has provided leadership in three award-winning school districts in two different states. His frontline experience includes positions as a teacher, counselor, supervisor, curriculum director, personnel director, associate superintendent, acting superintendent, and adjunct professor.

Ramsey knows about fiscal fitness through hands-on experience in stretching resources, cutting budgets, closing schools, and laying off personnel in an inner-ring suburban school system. Despite significant belt-tightening, this same school district still managed to become the first in the country where every elementary and secondary school was recognized by the federal government as a National School of Excellence.

Ramsey now works full time as a freelance writer in Minneapolis. Throughout his distinguished career, his writings, including the popular *Lead, Follow, or Get Out of the Way,* have helped countless teachers, principals, and superintendents to reach their full potential. In this latest book, his practical advice and school-ready suggestions can help any administrator make the most of all available resources and do even more with less.

Introduction

Coming to Grips With Reality

Let's face it. No matter how wealthy your school or school district is, your slice of the pie never seems like enough. Have you ever known a principal or superintendent who thought that he or she had all the resources needed to do the job?

Unfortunately, the pie is not going to get significantly bigger. And your knowing how to ask for a larger piece may not be enough to help your school succeed.

When you look around, however, you see that some school leaders make their share go a lot further than others. How do they do that? Do they have a magic formula? Have they found some kind of "Hamburger Helper" for school budgets? The answer is—none of the above.

The truth is that most schools, yours included, already have what they need in order to achieve their goals. Their piece of the pie is big enough after all. What's needed is for school leaders to figure out how to use all they have to the fullest. This book can help. And although it all starts by coming to grips with fiscal realities, the good news is that it doesn't cost anything to get real.

Why Schools Today Have to Do More With Less

It is OK to hope for a windfall for your school. In the meantime, you better start chasing extra change and learning how to get more out of your school's existing budget, personnel, equipment, and supplies.

In today's real world, schools are increasingly being called on to maximize the use of every available resource and, sometimes, to do more with less. This is not going to get any better any time soon. Here's why:

1. School bashing is gaining momentum. Everyone (except, of course, those students, parents, and teachers who are directly involved and know what is going on) seems to be joining the chorus of condemnation for the public schools' perceived shortfalls. In the words of many critics, "Why throw good money after bad and invest more in a system that's not working?"

2. Competition is getting stiffer. Alternative educational delivery systems are siphoning off more and more funds that otherwise might have ended up in your school's budget. As such options as voucher systems, charter schools, and home schooling gain in popularity, regular public schools have to make do with and make the most of present resources—or if they are lucky, of present resources plus modest increases.

3. A growing number of states and school districts are penalizing individual schools for perceived failings (e.g., low test scores). The idea is to withhold support from schools that are having trouble. How that is supposed to help remains a mystery to many educators. Nevertheless, the trend could mean reduced resources for your school.

4. Many states face ongoing lawsuits challenging the legality of their basic educational funding formulas. Until states figure out how they can, must, and want to finance education, funding for schools is likely to remain in limbo.

5. Escalating teacher shortages are making it difficult (sometimes impossible) for schools to hire all the teachers they need, particularly in specialized areas such as math, science, computer science, industrial technology, and special education. Record low unemployment rates mean qualified teachers now have unlimited employment options—many of which lie outside the field of education. Obviously, the challenge of the new millennium for school leaders is to find ways to do more with less personnel (see Chapter 2).

6. School facilities are being used longer hours for more months out of the year by more community groups than ever before. The physical plants in most schools are being strained to the limit. It is a no-brainer that school leaders now have to get more out of existing buildings and mechanical systems.

7. Likewise, age is taking its toll on the infrastructure of many schools. Much of America has old schools. This means that educators have to extend the life of their buildings and, probably, spend money on bricks and mortar that could have been spent on kids. If there is anything harder than stretching existing resources, it is stretching existing old resources.

8. New school construction costs too much. Whenever schools have to build new facilities, school budgets take a hit. Guess what that means? Saving money and being more efficient elsewhere. It's called fiscal fitness.

9. The cost of keeping up with technological advancements is crippling some school budgets. Schools have to stay current; but if there is no new money, the resources have to come from somewhere else. It is going to be up to school administrators like yourself to figure out how to make it work.

10. Expectations will continue to exceed available resources. Even if budgets are increased, needs and ideas for spending will grow faster. There will always be more hands held out than there are dollars coming in. That is why today's school leaders have to be better at creative resource management than their predecessors.

It does not take a very sophisticated trend-spotter to determine that to be successful in the future, administrators will have to find ways to educate kids faster, better, and cheaper. It's a new role for many.

The Role of the Principal in Hard Times

Demanding times demand new strands of leadership. In addition to their traditional functions (i.e., managing, supervising, vision-building, disciplining, coaching, cheerleading, and teaching teachers), times of tight resources now require that school administrators become *prospectors.*

Today's principals and superintendents need a radar for resources. Because of continuing downsizing, budget cuts, and fiscal restraints, educational leaders now often have to scratch and claw for resources sufficient to maintain and improve school programs. Through non-traditional fundraising, creative reallocations of resources, and aggressive partnering with businesses and other organizations, educators have to discover or invent new ways to supplement normal funding sources. *Resourcefulness* has taken on a whole new meaning for today's school administrators. This is one more good reason for reading this book.

What to Do in Times of Cost Containment

School administrators have always been good at spending money. They know how to create new positions, add staff, develop new programs, and buy all the latest educational gadgetry and paraphernalia. When it comes to "unspending" (e.g., cost containment, cutting back or reallocating resources), however, many principals and superintendents don't have a clue as to what to do. It's a new experience for many, and it's not covered in "principal's school."

Hard times hit all organizations. Schools can be particularly vulnerable to budget reversals because of their dependency on the tax dollars and mood swings of a fickle public and elected bodies. Sooner or later, every school official has to deal with times of financial constraint, belt-tightening, and/or retrenchment.

Conserving resources and cost cutting do not happen without leadership. That's your job. In hard times, the role of the principal or superintendent is to help maintain perspective and to prevent fiscal setbacks and shortages of resources from devastating the organization. No matter how bad the budget news is, the business of the school must go on and students must continue to receive the best possible education within available resources.

Cost containment should not be allowed to become all time-consuming. The best approach is to be as creative and upbeat as possible. Good things can come out of troubled economic conditions. Just because belt-tightening or reductions are necessary doesn't mean that some things can't be improved at the same time.

The first steps are to search for new ways of doing things and to look for efficiencies as well as for cuts. Money saved through economies now means fewer outright cutbacks in the long run.

In implementing any fiscal fitness process, it is always helpful to develop alternative scenarios involving a variety of action plans. Be realistic. Don't waste time considering any cuts or trade-offs that really can't be made because of existing mandates, contractual commitments, legal requirements, or local sentiment.

In most cases, the sooner cuts are made, the better because of the cumulative impact over time (e.g., $1,000 saved this year adds up to $2,000 in savings by the end of the second year).

Understanding and support are crucial to surviving hard times. If anything, effective communication is more important in difficult times than when things are going well. Keeping the lines of communication open and operating is part of your job as the school leader.

One of the essential messages you need to make sure gets heard is that less can be enough. Sometimes less is even better, if properly handled. The truth is that you can reduce almost anything, except your expectations, and still come out on top.

The Upside of Downsizing

"Total freedom is meaningless—obligations give us the chance to matter."

—Dr. Laura Schlessinger

Cost containment is neither universally good nor universally bad. It's what you make of it.

Good times, handled badly, can lead to bad results. Prosperity isn't always kind to us. A fat budget is one of the leading causes of sloth in both individuals and organizations. Excess also tends to foster arrogance, rather than accountability.

Hard times, handled well, can spawn positive outcomes. Challenge produces champions. Initiating a program of fiscal fitness can be the greatest thing that ever happened to your school. It's really up to you.

In the best organizations, there is always an upside to downsizing if it is undertaken for a good reason. The goal should be to reinvent the organization, making it tighter, stronger, and more efficient. When that happens, the school is positioned for greater success than ever.

A leaner, meaner organization promotes improved productivity and greater efficiency. That means a better learning environment for kids. That's the kind of school you've wanted all along.

Schools that survive a period of belt-tightening usually find they have a stronger, more cohesive unit than before. Best of all, faculties and staffs, which come through a rigorous program of fiscal fitness together, often boast greater confidence, loyalty, and mutual respect. These are the qualities that great schools are made of. And they are all free. Who says less isn't more?

What Smaller, Less Affluent Schools Have Known All Along

Many rural educators and administrators of small schools never feel envious of their bigger and richer counterparts in the cities and suburbs. In fact, they believe they have the advantage.

To succeed, large metropolitan and urban schools count on more course offerings, larger faculties with a higher percentage of them holding advanced degrees, and fancier facilities. Smaller, less affluent schools have to bank on intimacy, personal attention, and first-hand knowledge of what individual students need in order to get the job done. Their way is cheaper and simpler. They may be on to something.

Have you ever noticed that as soon as some affluent school district builds another expansive educational edifice capable of accommodating thousands of students, they immediately start looking for ways to make it function more like a small school? They often divert huge sums to hire cadres of counselors and to develop house plans, schools within a school, homeroom activities, and advisor-advisee programs, all in an attempt to recapture some of the closeness and personalization that smaller schools have had all along. Maybe bigger isn't better after all.

It isn't glitter or glitz, the size of the campus, the number of course offerings, or the pedigrees of the pedagogues that make a winning school. It's the level of support for individual learners and the quality of teacher-pupil interaction that matter most.

You won't find these components in the school budget. They don't cost a lot or consume a lot of other resources. Any school can afford them. Leaders of rural schools, small schools, and less affluent schools have known this all along. It's a lesson that the need for greater fiscal fitness is now revealing to the rest of us.

Simplification Is Catching On

There's a growing grassroots movement to simplify America. It is gaining momentum in businesses, government, religious institutions, schools, and the personal everyday lives of people all across the country.

The signs of simplification are everywhere—here are a few:

- The enormous popularity of recent best-sellers such as Elaine St. James's *Simplify Your Life* and *Inner Simplicity*
- Growing efforts to reinvent government along simpler lines
- The flattening of traditional hierarchical organizational charts in increasing numbers of public and private sector organizations
- The widespread downsizing of corporations in all fields
- The countless men and women resigning high-profile executive positions in order to live a less frenetic lifestyle

In education, the indications of a swing toward simplification include nationwide attempts to declutter school bureaucracies, procedures, and curriculum, to eliminate waste in school operations, and to heighten the efficiency and productivity of school personnel.

Individuals and organizations at all levels are embracing simplicity because they want to reconnect with their true values and actually live their priorities. It can work that way for schools as well.

Simplification and fiscal fitness go hand in hand. They're catching on. It's a trend you don't want to miss out on.

The Angler and the Executive

A Parable

A businessman was standing at the pier of a small Mexican coastal village when a small boat with a single fisherman pulled up to the dock. Inside the boat were several tuna. He complimented the man on his catch and asked how long it took to catch them.

"Not long," the fisherman replied.

When the businessman asked why he didn't stay longer to catch more, the fisherman said he had caught enough to take care of his family for the next few days.

"But what do you do with the rest of your time?" the businessman wanted to know.

"I sleep late, fish a little, play with my children, take siesta with my wife, and then stroll each evening into the village to sing and play guitar with my amigos."

The businessman offered to help the man's fishing business grow. Step one would be catching more fish. The man could then buy a larger boat and, ultimately, a fleet. He could sell directly to the processor and eventually raise enough capital to open his own cannery.

As a tycoon, he would want to move to New York, where he could preside over his fishing empire. Of course, this would all take 15 to 20 years of hard work.

"But the sacrifice will be worth it," the businessman assured him. After all, once the fisherman issued an IPO for his enterprise, he'd be rich.

"Then what?" wondered the fisherman.

"You'd be able to retire and live the good life. You can move to a small coastal village, where you would sleep late, fish a little, play with your kids, take siestas with your wife, and stroll in the evenings to the village, where you could sing and play guitar with your amigos."

From the Internet; author unknown.

How to Use This Handbook

The times of tight school budgets and never-quite-enough resources are here to stay. Deal with it. It's OK to moan, but it's better to become aggressive in managing fiscal realities to your school's advantage.

This book tells you how. It's filled with tools to help your school get in shape to deal with any period of economizing, cost containment, or retrenchment.

The guide can be read from cover to cover as a basic text on fiscal fitness for schools. It is more valuable, however, as a reference resource that can be visited again and again, like a favorite cookbook is a source for new food ideas and proved recipes. Anytime you need help with raising funds, cutting costs, stretching program dollars, getting more out of present personnel, and any other resource management problem, a wealth of ideas and strategies are available right here, right at your fingertips.

Fiscal Fitness for School Administrators is also useful for what it doesn't say. Every list of school-ready solutions contained in this text is bound to trigger a rush of additional possibilities that suit your unique situation. Feel free to use the handbook as both a primer and a pump-primer. You can't ask for much more than that.

There are a lot of great ideas in every chapter that follows. But that's where they will stay, unless you dig them out and begin applying them. It turns out that fiscal fitness is a do-it-yourself project. A really good time to start is right now.

1

How to Cut Costs Without Cutting Essential Programs and Services

Human organizations sometimes take on negative human characteristics, such as sloth, sloppiness, self-absorption, and self-aggrandizement. Institutions can also acquire expensive tastes just as people do. That's why many organizations, including schools, often pick up excess baggage in the form of extra purposes, priorities, practices, procedures, personnel, perks, and paraphernalia that they don't really need. With each addition, the organization grows bigger, more complex, more bureaucratic, and more costly.

Spending is a habit. Economizing and frugality are also habits. Fortunately, habits can be learned and unlearned. Individuals can become more disciplined in how they handle resources. Institutions can, too. They're usually better off for the effort. You start by changing the way you think about what's really important and what you're going to do about it.

Fiscal Fitness Is an Attitude

As long as schools think that they have to do more, offer more, have more, and be more to be better, they will never break the pattern of spiraling costs. But once a school's staff starts thinking and talking about economizing and efficiency, cost containment can quickly become a way of life. To stretch school resources, live within their means, and still get the job done, schools have to adopt a "brass tacks" attitude toward fiscal fitness.

Most personal trainers agree that attaining physical fitness is as much a matter of attitude as of diet and exercise. Fiscal fitness is the same. With the right mental attitude, doing more with less is possible in any school. Fiscal fitness can become an attitude that drives decision making throughout the school and serves as a filter for making choices that shape programs and services.

To catch on, an attitude of cost containment and fiscal responsibility should be rooted in a no-nonsense belief system that is accepted and internalized by the staff, such as the following 12 "We Believe That . . . " statements:

We Believe That . . .

1. More isn't necessarily better.
2. All kids can learn and we can teach them.
3. A good education doesn't have to cost an arm and a leg.
4. Focused instruction is better than random teaching.
5. Education, like sports, is largely a matter of mastering fundamentals.
6. Schools can identify a manageable mission and stick to it.
7. Good teaching requires good teachers, not fancy gimmickry.
8. Curriculum, materials, methods, and relationships determine the conditions of learning. Of these four, relationships are the most important.
9. Any school that believes in kids and believes in itself can accomplish wonders on a shoestring.
10. Setbacks are merely opportunities for comebacks—the right response to a setback is renewed effort.
11. Without problems, there would be no possibility for triumph.
12. People make it happen.

What the school staff believes is what the school becomes. When people act on their beliefs, those beliefs come to life. Perceptions really are reality. As do other human organizations, schools respond to self-fulfilling prophecies. It isn't the size of the budget that marks the difference between a winning school and a losing school. It's attitude.

Of course, attitudes don't just happen. The mood and mindset of any school are greatly influenced by the principal. If the leader adopts an attitude of fiscal restraint, the staff is likely to follow. That's how fiscal fitness can become the accepted way of doing business in the school.

It's the principal's job to keep reminding staff, students, parents, and the community of what's really important and what is possible— not necessarily of what costs the most.

What Matters Most Costs the Least

Fiscal fitness requires putting things into perspective, sorting out what matters most, and establishing clearcut priorities that everyone understands.

New band uniforms are nice; but they don't teach music any better. Compact discs are cool; but cassette tapes do the same job for less. This year's textbook editions look better; but last year's have essentially the same information. Fiscal fitness is focusing on what really counts and refusing to be distracted by fluff and glitz.

Of all the blue-ribbon schools across the country that have been recognized by the federal government as national schools of excellence, as many come from inner cities or modest middle-class neighborhoods as from affluent suburbs. Money doesn't make the difference. Surprisingly, the things that make up a truly great school aren't big-ticket items. What matters most often costs the least.

High expectations, challenging assignments, authentic teaching, a caring environment, rigorous standards, commitment to excellence, meaningful dialogue, firm and fair discipline, second chances, pride in accomplishment, hard work, positive reinforcement, seriousness of purpose, trust, honest feedback, respect for individual differences, excitement for learning, and old-fashioned fun don't cost a lot. In fact, they're mostly free.

These are the building blocks of fiscal fitness. By valuing, nurturing, and concentrating on these elements instead of on a lot of trappings that don't make a difference, your school can make the most of all available resources and do even more with less.

Once a genuine "do more with less" attitude and belief system are in place, the first exercise in any school's fiscal fitness regimen is to cut costs without cutting essential programs and services. Many well-meaning cost containment efforts fail or never even get off the

It Doesn't Cost Anything To . . .

Work smarter
Be fair
Ask tougher questions
Listen more
Expect students to do
    "real" work
Refuse to inflate grades
Celebrate successes
Stay up-to-date
Break down stereotypes
Set routines
Vary activities more often
Try harder
Care more
Support student dreams
Believe in kids
Involve parents more
Get better organized

Keep reading to kids of
    all ages
Build on strengths
Help each other more
Practice amnesty
Model civility
Be a stickler for details
Take students seriously
Hug kids who need it
Seek and give feedback
Treat all kids alike—fairly
Expect students to give
    their best
Be the best you can be
Be honest with students
Be passionate about teaching
Smile more
Always put children first
Have more fun with kids

Who says you can't do more with less?

ground because the principal and staff don't know or can't agree on where to start or how to proceed.

The secret is to begin by determining what stays rather than what goes. The first step is to identify what you're going to keep at all costs.

Four Things Your School Has to Do
in Good Times and Bad

No matter how tight the budget becomes, there are certain functions your school must perform or it ceases to be a viable educational

delivery system. These essential activities need to be spelled out so that they can be protected. That's why schools have mission statements. Knowing what has to be preserved makes it easier to identify what can be reduced or eliminated.

Schools describe these nonnegotiable functions in different ways. The most succinct statements of the critical things all schools have to do are contained in the 1995 report from the Carnegie Foundation for the Advancement of Teaching and Learning:

1. Agree on and teach a core of math, science, and language, then measure the results.
2. Create a sense of community, stressing discipline and caring for children, while reaching out to parents and local businesses.
3. Provide health, counseling, and other services for children, and find a way to provide resources such as books, maps, computers, and phone lines.
4. Teach children about ethics along with academics.

These are the basics your school has to provide no matter what. (How you do it is up to you and your staff.) In good times or bad, effective schools do whatever it takes to shield these functions. These are givens and are off limits in times of budget reduction. Everything else is optional. Cost cutting, then, is simply a process of getting rid of nonessentials, no matter how popular or appealing they may be.

Peeling the Onion

After an onion has been around for awhile, the outer skins begin to dry out, turn brown, shrivel up, and become brittle. The flavor and aroma go too. They no longer serve any purpose for cooking or eating. That's why good cooks always peel away the outer layers to get to the sweet, pungent core where the real taste is.

Schools aren't onions; but the metaphor is obvious. After years of operation, many schools become enveloped in layer upon layer of bureaucracy, rules, rituals, procedures, and protocol. Many of these layers no longer serve any real purpose for learning. Some even may have become defunct long ago; but they never drop away by themselves.

Cost cutting in schools is similar to peeling an onion. The outer layers that no longer serve a direct educational purpose need to be stripped away to get to the viable inner core. The trick is to peel away only the redundant or useless layers and to avoid peeling off any more than necessary. The object is to preserve as much of the healthy core as possible.

This means that school officials can't just hack away randomly at the budget during periods of retrenchment. Effective budget reduction requires a plan. It's easier than you may think. If you do it right, you can end up doing more with less.

Guidelines, Considerations, and Criteria for Making School Budget Reductions

Fiscal fitness requires tough-minded decision making. Such decisions aren't whims or snap judgments. They need to be based on valid input from multiple sources and carefully weighed against predetermined priorities, criteria, and reality checks. Good cost containment decisions aren't made in a vacuum. They must be reached within the context of an overall strategy for achieving fiscal fitness.

Budget reductions are always painful; but having a plan can help. These guidelines and suggestions have guided many school leaders in making difficult retrenchment decisions, while preserving (and sometimes enhancing) essential programs and services:

- The ultimate goal of any budget reduction effort should be to retain a viable educational program (the things that all schools have to do in good times and bad), to preserve the capability to fulfill the school's mission, and to maximize instructional opportunities for all learners.

- Cost containment should include a combination of program reduction, elimination, reallocation, economies, efficiencies, savings, and revenue production.

- The school's vision, mission, belief statements, and program goals should determine budget priorities.

- Start early. Have a time line and stick to it.

- Involve as many stakeholders as possible. All stakeholders should be afforded an opportunity to suggest cuts, savings, economies, and revenue-raising proposals and to react to tentative reduction plans before final implementation. Final decisions, however, should be left to those who can be held accountable (i.e., principal and staff).

- Be open, honest, and upfront throughout the process. Don't make promises that you may not be able to keep.

- Establish ground rules for participation in the process (no finger pointing, no whining, etc.).

- Avoid simplistic across-the-board reductions. Not all programs are equal.

- Cut first as far away from instruction (the classroom) as possible.

- Cut things before people; but don't kid yourself. Significant savings may necessitate personnel cutbacks or layoffs.

- All areas and programs should be subject to scrutiny with survival depending on merit.

- Consider long-term as well as short-term impacts of all cuts under consideration.

- Respect contractual obligations. All reductions must be allowable under current, existing contracts. Remember that seniority provisions often dictate the order of any layoffs.

- Accept reality. Increasing class size may be the only way to achieve needed budget reductions.

- Consider revenue-raising measures, along with budget reductions.

- Look for efficiencies before effecting more drastic economies or cutbacks.

- Ask if programs or services can be scaled back, rather than eliminated completely.

- Don't be fooled into thinking that some cuts will be completely painless. Every retrenchment has impact. There is an advocate somewhere for every program who will complain, claim foul, and feel slighted if reductions occur.

- Weigh any negative impact on other schools or programs when considering specific reductions in your own.

- Realize that the administration will be everybody's "whipping boy." Administration may be cut; but always retain sufficient leadership to carry on business with surviving programs and services.
- Preserve enough public relations and communication capability to be able to tell the school's story throughout the reduction process and beyond.
- Give first priority to reductions that can be carried out within the preferred or projected time frame.
- Strive to make reductions that are politically acceptable to the community.
- Don't be afraid to consider reductions in programs that are partially reimbursed by the state or federal government, such as special education or vocational education.
- Make it clear that budget reductions do not preclude new initiatives when they are needed and appropriate.
- Realize that timing is important. Procrastination is no friend of fiscal fitness. Budget problems don't get better by themselves. Undue delays now may only mean deeper cuts later on.
- Identify more cuts than you need. If things get worse, you don't want to have to start all over.

No guidelines can make cost reduction feel good; but it always feels better when you know you've done it right. Once appropriate guidelines and criteria have been established, it's time to bite the bullet. When difficult budget cuts are called for, effective principals put off procrastination. It won't get easier. It may get worse. Just do it.

A Step-by-Step Budget Reduction Process That Really Works

Using these or similar guidelines, schools have to design their own methodology for making budget reductions. The quality of the product depends on the quality of the process.

A sound cost-containment process is thorough, methodical, inclusive, and timely. Any procedure for reducing expenses must include a realistic timetable. It should take as long as needed to be done right, but no longer than necessary, to avoid protracting the agony.

The kind of step-by-step budget reduction process outlined here has proven successful in many winning schools and can work in your school as well.

Steps in Budget Reduction

1. Identify a realistic budget-reduction target figure. This amount often is simply the school's share of an overall district-wide reduction goal. Build in a modest cushion if possible.

2. Agree on a workable timetable. The school's budget reduction calendar must mesh with the district's fiscal year and time line.

3. If needed, form a building-level fiscal fitness steering committee made up of a cross section of stakeholders. The size of the school usually determines whether or not such a group is necessary or desirable.

4. Reach agreement among stakeholders on criteria and guidelines to be followed throughout the process.

5. Communicate the agreed-on process and timetable to all stakeholders.

6. Involve staff (all employees) and other stakeholders (students, parents, advisory committees, site councils, PTA, etc.) in generating—brainstorming—a list of proposed cost-cutting and revenue-raising recommendations. Each recommendation must include an estimate of the anticipated savings or added revenue. Some schools find it useful the first time around to limit individuals and groups to recommending reductions in their own programs or areas of responsibility, rather than proposing cuts in other people's programs.

7. Share the complete list of preliminary recommendations with the district office and the school board (if appropriate) for initial review, comment, and tentative approval (if required).

8. Review tentative recommendations with stakeholders and revise as appropriate.

9. Use discussion and/or a forced-choice procedure for reaching consensus on prioritized cost-containment recommendations.

10. Finalize the school's fiscal fitness plan. Refine all estimates of savings and new revenues.

11. Share the final plan with stakeholders and the community. Stress any positive effects. Reaffirm all that has been retained.

12. Implement recommendations without whining or apologizing. Evaluate results. Save all discarded suggestions for the next round of cost containment.

Note: Applicable legal time lines, benchmark events, and notification requirements must be followed if layoffs (terminations) are to be part of the cost-containment package. Specific requirements vary from state to state and should be incorporated into the school's budget reduction process and calendar.

It can't be stressed too strongly that timeliness is critical in any fiscal fitness effort. If the process is rushed, important possibilities may be overlooked or consequences may not be thoroughly considered. If the process takes too long, opportunities may be missed and the situation may grow even worse. That's why savvy principals pay as much attention to the timetable of the budget reduction process as to the steps involved.

A Sample Budget Reduction Calendar

It's the principal's responsibility to see that the school's budget reduction plans come in on target and on time. Few school deadlines are irrevocable. The cutoff date for budget reductions is one of them. Don't miss it.

This prototype calendar can serve as a model for ensuring that fiscal fitness—stretching resources and doing more with less—becomes a reality in your school.

Budget Reduction Calendar

October	Identify targeted reduction amount.
	Develop budget reduction process, timetable, and guidelines.
November	Begin generating fiscal fitness suggestions and priorities. Create as many opportunities and means for receiving suggestions as possible, including small group meetings, public hearings, a fiscal fitness hot line, an e-mail address, a dedicated voice mailbox, and provisions for written suggestions (see Form 1.1).
December	Continue stakeholder discussions and revisions of preliminary recommendations.
January	Conduct further staff and public hearings on tentative budget reductions.
February	Finalize the school's fiscal fitness recommendations.
	Communicate completed plan to all interested and involved parties.
March	Begin implementation of cost-containment measures.
	Initiate unrequested leave (termination) process if applicable.
April and May	Complete unrequested leave placement if appropriate.
June	Complete staffing and final plans for the coming school year using the reconfiguration of programs and services.

Developing a comfortable calendar or manageable schedule for achieving fiscal fitness is only half the battle. A timetable is good only if you stick to it.

If you don't complete your fiscal fitness exercise on time, someone else (i.e., district office administrators or the school board) may do it for you. Having to cut costs in your own school is bad. Having someone else do the budgetary surgery on your school is worse. If you want it done right, do it yourself—on time!

Form 1.1. Cost-Containment Suggestion Form

Cost-Containment Suggestion Form

Date: _____

Directions: Complete a separate form for each suggestion.

1. Cost-Containment Suggestion

   Program, department, or service: _____

   Describe your suggestion: _____

   _____

   _____

   _____

   Estimated amount saved/revenue raised by this suggestion: $ _____

2. Student Impact Statement

   If your suggestion is adopted, what is the *best* that would happen for students? _____

   _____

   _____

   _____

   If your suggestion is adopted, what is the *worst* that would happen for students? _____

   _____

   _____

   _____

   Submitted by: _____

How to Encourage Early Retirements

Schools are labor-intensive organizations. When serious budget reductions have to be made, some personnel adjustments are inevitable. It's the only way schools can pick up substantive savings. A big part of stretching resources is often doing more with fewer people (see Chapter 2). This is particularly true in times of teacher shortages.

Attrition is always the best way to reduce staff. The involuntary termination of staff members takes a little longer and hurts a lot more. Layoffs leave wounds that heal very slowly, if at all. That's why it pays to encourage eligible staff members to consider early retirement whenever it becomes necessary to shrink the school's workforce.

As principal, you don't want anyone on your staff to feel undervalued, unappreciated, or unwanted. Likewise, you don't want any employees to feel that they are being pushed out; but you do want your staff members to make choices and decisions based on full information and complete understanding of the situation.

There's nothing wrong with seeing to it that all senior staff members are aware of the benefits available to them through your state's teacher retirement system and your district's severance package for early retirees. This information should be provided in good times as well as in periods of potential layoffs.

You also have an obligation to be sure that potential early retirees realize they have an opportunity to save the job of a junior colleague if they choose to do so. What they do with the information is up to them.

One way to encourage early retirements is through an information memo to senior staff members as shown in the example on the next page. Such a memo is most effective when a union representative co-signs it. Retirement seminars, on-site retirement counseling, and presentations by recent retirees are other effective ways to urge early retirees to come forward in a timely manner.

Early retirement can be a win-win situation for everyone—the retiree, the person whose job is saved, and the school as a whole.

When personnel reductions are imminent, encourage attrition in any way you can; but at the same time, be prepared to effect involuntary layoffs if necessary.

Example:
Memo Encouraging Early Retirements

Memo to: Senior Staff Members

Subject: Early Retirement Considerations

The purpose of this memo is to encourage all senior staff members who are eligible and who are considering early retirement at the end of the current school year to make a commitment as soon as possible and to submit early notification of intent to retire if that is their decision.

As we all know, some staff positions will have to be eliminated for next year. Unless reductions can be realized through attrition, layoffs are inevitable. Every confirmed retirement will ease the situation.

We are all familiar with the anxieties our colleagues experience when they are faced with the possibility of being placed on unrequested leave. You can help avoid this stress by declaring your intent to retire by February 1, 20___. Such action on your part can save the job and reduce the anxiety and worry of a junior friend and coworker.

If you have questions about your early retirement options, please feel free to contact either one of us or the human resources department at any time. It may also be helpful to review the early retirement incentives contained in the master contract and/or to check your pension status with the state's teachers retirement association.

Please give serious consideration to declaring your intent to retire by February 1, 20___ so that unnecessary layoffs can be avoided.

_____   _____

Principal   (Teacher Union Representative)

How to Ease the Pain of Layoffs

If you can find enough ways to make the most of all resources and/or do more with less without cutting personnel, do it. Chances are, you can't. The next best thing is if retirements, resignations, and transfers take care of any necessary reductions in staff. If that doesn't happen, you may have no choice but to terminate some employees. When you do have to lay off personnel, at least do it right. Be direct; be honest; be fair; and be swift. Bad news doesn't get better with delay.

Layoffs can have several damaging effects on the school, such as lower morale, strained relationships, loss of trust, reduced performance, and interstaff conflicts. These effects may even carry over into the classroom. Of even greater concern may be the negative impacts on affected individuals, which often include grieving, loss of self-esteem, economic hardships, fear, stress, and depression. All of these factors must be taken into account whenever you are engineering a series of staff reductions.

Implementing a program of staff retrenchment should be more than a numbers game. It can and should be a human process. The practical suggestions that follow have succeeded in many schools to help minimize negative impacts, to ease the trauma for those involved, to preserve a human focus during a difficult period, and to maintain the quality of relationships and performance throughout the school. The following steps can ease the pain of layoffs in your school as well:

- Plan ahead. Provide projected staff needs (on a department-by-department basis if possible) as early as possible.
- Don't keep secrets. Be upfront about cutback plans.
- Make public all pertinent information (i.e., projected enrollments, budget figures, seniority lists).
- Involve the staff in developing cost-containment and staff-reduction recommendations whenever possible.
- Keep the educational program paramount throughout the process.
- Humanize and personalize the notification process as much as you can. Deliver layoff notices in person, in private.
- Provide outplacement services and assistance where possible.

- Be diligent and timely in providing references and recommendations for staff members who are laid off.
- Provide information about outstanding teachers and other employees affected by layoffs to other schools that may need to add qualified personnel.
- Be flexible in allowing terminated staff members to participate in job interviews during the regular workday.
- Don't take personally the natural anger and resentment expressed by terminated employees.
- Take safety precautions in case any terminated employees react violently.
- Involve affected employees in midcareer-change workshops when feasible.
- Focus on the healing process. Emphasize the positive effects of change.

In our economy being laid off is no longer an uncommon experience. It happens in all fields and professions. People learn to deal with it. Fortunately, there are a lot of different jobs in education. Most employees who are laid off for reasons beyond their control will find one of them. For those who don't, many will make successful and exciting career changes. There is life after layoff. Downsizing is never fun, but it's seldom fatal.

Although reducing staff is painful, it can be healthy for the organization in the long run. Fewer people doesn't necessarily mean diminished performance or less success. You may be surprised to find out that you can run as good a school, and sometimes even a better school, with less staff. Chapter 2 explains how to do it.

2

How to Accomplish As Much or More With Less Staff

Education is a people business. Many schools and school districts expend as much as 70% to 80% of their budgets on personnel. That makes schools labor intensive and labor expensive.

If you want or need to stretch school resources, cut costs, increase efficiency, streamline operations, or do more with less, you have to do something differently with people. In schools you can cut everything else to the bone; but if you don't affect people, you won't make a difference.

The only real ways for school administrators to achieve maximum cost-effectiveness are to reduce the number of people on the payroll, deploy personnel more efficiently, or get more out of existing staff. Some school officials maintain that achieving maximum cost-effectiveness cannot be done. If you're reading this book, you're probably not one of them.

Despite what some say, you can accomplish as much or more with less staff. This chapter will tell you how. But it won't happen if you stick with traditional thinking.

Practice Creative Staffing

Some of today's most influential business gurus are so committed to the "science of doing more with less people" that they are now hiring "knowledge engineers" to help them incorporate job-related knowledge and expertise into software systems that can, then, do some of the work of human beings.

27

There's not much chance that software or artificial intelligence will replace teachers; but school leaders can take a cue from their business counterparts. It pays to evaluate your organization to determine what opportunities and possibilities exist. Creative staffing can help you get the job done faster, better, and cheaper.

There's more than one way to staff a school. There's even a better way to staff yours—if you are persistent and inventive enough to find it.

It may not be as hard as you think. Many schools already have a track record of finding better ways to use human resources. Some have implemented a variety of differentiated staffing models. Others have worked through site councils to trade off professional positions for more teacher aide and support positions. A lot of creative staffing has occurred and is occurring in schools everywhere; but there is more to be done. Isn't it time you got in on the action?

If yours is like most schools, the staffing level for teachers is set by a time-honored formula that divides the number of pupils enrolled by a predetermined (arbitrary) number. This is a simple, clean, and clear way to define the school's teacher-pupil ratio and identify the number of full-time equivalents (FTEs) to be employed. But it's only one way to do it. There are others. Some may be better.

What would happen if you changed the formula? Or made up a new one? Or didn't use a cut-and-dried formula at all?

Don't stick with old formulas or staffing patterns just because it's always been done that way. You might find a better way if you only look. Keep looking.

You can start anytime. There's an opportunity to start practicing creative staffing any time a vacancy occurs.

Use Openings As Opportunities

Most human resource professionals agree that there are five basic strategies for changing the way you employ, deploy, or use people in your organization:

1. Eliminate
2. Automate
3. Educate

   4. Delegate

   5. Reallocate

Of these, reallocation is often the easiest and most effective method of staffing more efficiently. This is especially true with administrative and support positions.

Every time a position opens up in your school, there is an opportunity to reallocate duties and responsibilities, save money, streamline functions, and, maybe, do the work even better for less. This is too good an opportunity to pass up.

Reallocate ought to be a frequently used word in your staff's everyday vocabulary. When vacancies occur, people at all levels of the organization should think first about the possibility of reallocation, then about filling the position as is. Don't ever automatically hire a replacement for any job without first reviewing the position for the possibilities of reallocating some or all of the responsibilities involved.

Never rush to fill positions. Many successful principals and superintendents make it a practice to hold vacancies open for at least two months to see if the functions can be performed as well or better by someone else or in some other way.

Some of the best examples of cost-saving reallocation involve clerical personnel. In many schools, all administrators, department heads, and supervisors have their own personal secretary. It's nice. It's part of the culture. It's tradition. It's expensive.

Some more cost-conscious schools are finding that they can reduce personnel and accomplish just as much or more for less by reallocating clerical duties and forming a secretarial pool that serves all administrators. It's one less perk for supervisory personnel; but it's one more point for fiscal fitness.

Reallocation works best when individual schools have greater control over their own human resources. District policies should include incentives for schools to reallocate and should never penalize individual efforts to find more creative staffing patterns.

Reallocation is a tool for effecting greater efficiency. But it doesn't always fit every situation. When it is necessary and appropriate to go ahead and fill an existing position without reallocating or changing it in any way, the next best thing you can do is hire someone with multiple skills and qualifications.

Hire for Flexibility

The more flexibility you have within your staff, the more options you have for stretching your human resources. That's why the best school leaders always hire with flexibility in mind. You should, too.

Hire personnel who can do more than one thing whenever possible. This means purposely looking for teachers with double majors and multiple licensure. It means filling staff positions in all categories with people who have broad backgrounds, varied skills, and more than one area of expertise. It also means cross-training employees at all levels of the organization once they are hired.

Obviously, you position yourself to get a much bigger bang for your buck when you hire people with combinations of talents. College football coaches are always looking for athletes who are double or triple threats, capable of playing many positions on both defense and offense. That's what makes winning teams. It can work for school staffs as well.

Following are some of the most common combinations to look for when building maximum flexibility into your team:

- Teachers who are also licensed as counselors and counselors who can teach
- Special education teachers who can work with multiple disabilities and disorders
- Foreign language teachers who are proficient in more than one language
- Custodians who can also perform security functions and even drive a school bus if needed
- Aides with teaching licensure and experience
- Teachers who can coach, preferably in more than one sport
- Elementary teachers with a second major in a foreign language (this combination will prove invaluable if you initiate an elementary foreign language program or a foreign language immersion program later on)
- Secretaries who have accounting and bookkeeping skills in addition to basic clerical skills
- Elementary and secondary teachers who are also licensed to teach at the middle school levels

It doesn't cost any more to hire people who are flexible, and it may save you money later on. Flexibility enables you to adopt different cost-effective staffing arrangements to meet changing needs.

Flexibility doesn't just occur. You have to make it happen. It starts with the hiring process.

How to Get More
Out of Your Staff

When you can't hire any more or fire any more, you have to work with what you have got. The bottom line is that doing more with the same or less staff means improving the productivity of all existing staff members. If you can get professionals and support staff alike to work harder, faster, longer, or smarter, you will break performance records and save money, too.

In sports, the most successful coaches are those who get the most out of their players. Coaches aren't smarter than administrators. The same thing can work for school leaders.

Winning administrators keep their staffs interested, charged up, focused, and working to capacity. They know how to get everyone in the organization to want to do and be their best. When that happens, employees not only come through with peak performances, they also give their jobs a greater share of their discretionary time. That's free labor.

Of course, you may think that your teachers and other staff members are already overworked, stressed out, and stretched to the limit. You may be convinced that they can't work any harder or do any more. Don't kid yourself. Every school staff is capable of greater productivity. Even yours. But how do you make it happen?

The best way to get the most out of people is to hire and keep the best people to start with. After that, many successful school leaders follow these six simple steps for getting their staffs to give 110%:

1. *Expect a lot to get a lot.* Most teachers know that expecting more from students often becomes a self-fulfilling prophecy. High expectations can transform all obstacles. What they don't always know is that it works with adults as well. Hold high standards. Model excellence. Your staff will surprise you (and themselves) by living up to your expectations.

2. *Remove obstacles.* That's what leadership is all about. Teachers and support personnel fail to live up to their potential for a number of different reasons—boredom, lack of challenge, limited or no growth opportunities, lack of respect, a sense of powerlessness, lack of leadership. If you remove these obstacles, you eliminate the excuses for lackluster performance. That's what your most successful colleagues do all the time.

3. *Treat people right.* How you treat people has more to do with the level of effort they exert than any other single factor. Give what you want to get. Nurture and develop individual talent. Let staff members make decisions about matters that affect them directly. (It's called empowerment.) Do all the little things that help staff members cope with balancing work and family (e.g., arrange for a dry cleaning pickup at school).

Pay attention to the needs of your entire staff. Support newcomers by assigning mentors and providing survival kits containing tested tips on teaching and classroom management. At the other end of the spectrum, help veteran staff members deal with burnout. (Often, burnout is not permanent. Sometimes, all that's needed is a 1- to 6-week get-away-from-it-all escape.)

Many effective educators say that the best way to treat staff at all levels is first to "never say never," then to practice these three additional "nevers":

- Never allow people to drift unattended, unsupervised, and unnoticed.
- Never keep people in the dark.
- Never take people for granted.

Caring for employees doesn't mean coddling them. Usually, the biggest favor you can do for staff members is to stretch and challenge them by holding out for tough standards. If you treat people right, they will treat you right—with loyalty and hard work.

4. *Give constant encouragement.* Be relentless in encouraging all employees. Work hard to give them the tools they need to succeed. Be a cheerleader. Demonstrate your confidence in their abilities. Show that you believe in them. Once they are convinced, they'll give you their best.

5. *Build morale.* Morale is still the cornerstone of productivity. It is especially important to keep morale high when times are low. Cultivate pride. Make a big deal out of the history, stories, and heroes of the organization. Celebrate successes. Spending time nurturing morale and attending to the culture and climate of the organization is always a cost-effective way to get the most out of your staff.

6. *Stress teamwork.* Continuously look for new possibilities to form meaningful teams. Most staff members tend to work harder as part of a team than they do as individuals. Teaming multiplies talent and effort at all levels of the organization.

Good things happen when school leaders stick with these strategies. The 25 strategies that follow are more examples of how a successful school leader can model, coach, coax, cajole, and encourage peak performances by every staff member every day:

- Define clear goals and give clear directions.
- Stress face-to-face communication. Don't hide behind voice mail and e-mail.
- Don't sit on bad news.
- Praise in public—criticize in private.
- Listen to the words of your staff and see the feelings behind the words. (Every day you have numerous opportunities to keep your mouth shut and listen to others. Take advantage of them.)
- Encourage creativity and risk taking.
- Do whatever it takes to provide your staff members with the training they need to do their jobs right.
- Be family-friendly. Encourage staff members to cover for each other so individuals can attend important school functions involving their children. Allow employees to use their sick leave to care for ill children. Respect employee privacy and family time.
- Let staff members choose their own rewards.
- Let everyone know what's expected, allowed, valued, and rewarded in the organization.
- Keep your promises and expect others to do the same.

- Give credit—accept blame.
- Make civility the way you do business.
- Enforce zero tolerance for intolerance, bigotry, discrimination, and harassment.
- Be honest—about everything, all the time.
- Be accessible.
- Squelch rumors in the making.
- Pay attention to ergonomics.
- Keep it simple. Make few rules, but make them stick.
- Do something for the community—together.
- Surprise people. Do something nice for no reason.
- Give every team or department some discretionary funds ("mad money").
- Buffer your staff from needless interruptions, interference, demands, and frivolous complaints.
- Adopt a user-friendly grievance procedure.
- Make *fun* a priority.

Champion performers have the capacity to reach deep inside to call forth hidden reserves of energy and courage. That's the way they win titles and set records. Groups of people can do the same thing. Calling on your staff's hidden reserves is an effective way to accomplish more with less.

Tap the Power of Part-Time Personnel

Many principals and other administrators shy away from using part-time employees. It's too bad. They're missing a bet.

Part-time staffers can give you greater flexibility and often save the organization significant amounts of money in salaries and fringe benefits. Best of all, you usually get more for your money from part-time personnel.

We all know of part-time teachers and other employees who put in many more hours than they are paid for. It's not unheard of for an employer to get full-time effort for half-time pay. It may not be necessary. It's probably not fair. But it's a great dollar-saving deal for the organization.

Relying on well-qualified part-time staff members who really want the job is an effective way to stretch human resources. Never hesitate to tap into the power of part-time personnel. In addition to being cost-effective, it provides a good opportunity to "try out" potential future full-time employees or to hang on to valued retirees a bit longer.

The benefits of employing part-time personnel can be realized in both the professional and the support staff. Some of the most common and effective ways to use less-than-full-time personnel include tandem teaching, job sharing, and telecommuting (home-based employees).

Schools need full-time staff members to provide consistency, build relationships, and cover all the bases. Mixing in part-time personnel, however, can help extend staffing dollars and get more done at less cost. Anytime is a good time for a part-time employee if it gets the job done and saves money at the same time.

Use Nonlicensed Personnel
to Do More With Less

In addition to the judicious use of part-time staffers, another practical budget-helper is the hiring of nonlicensed personnel where appropriate, instead of paying top dollar for a certified professional. Although the unions will complain and traditionalists may cry foul, the truth is that some nonlicensed community members with specialized backgrounds and expertise can do certain jobs in the school as well as or better than the professionals on your regular staff.

When a layperson is the best choice for a particular job or task, dare to hire him or her. There's nothing wrong with hiring the best person available at a fraction of the cost of a professional's salary. Some might even call it good stewardship and sound management.

A good place to start capitalizing on the cost-effectiveness of nonlicensed personnel is to bring in professionals-in-the-making wherever possible and feasible. For instance, student teachers and administrative interns can be valuable additions to any school at no extra cost. When a talented student teacher helps a child or a group of children to read better, the students probably don't know or care that the teacher is not licensed.

Some of the most popular positions for nonlicensed staff are coaches (see the following guidelines), activity advisors, and lay readers. Share the cost of a police liaison officer with city government instead of assigning professional educators to security duty. Allow the city's forester or naturalist to teach science units on plants or animals (at no cost). Who on your staff could do it better?

Guidelines for Nonfaculty Coaches and Advisors

Nonfaculty coaches and advisors must place special emphasis on building relationships and on becoming familiar with philosophy and goals of the athletic and activity programs by:

1. Meeting with the principal and athletic director prior to the start of the season or activity for orientation and goal setting.
2. Calling the principal's or athletic director's office as determined on a prearranged schedule.
3. Holding periodic conferences with the principal and athletic director.
4. Following all procedures outlined in the coach's or advisor's job description.
5. Setting aside a regular time to meet individually with assistants and student participants.
6. Conferring with the principal or athletic director during the last week of the season or activity to plan for awards presentations, year-end reviews, and equipment check-in.
7. Being loyal to the school's traditions and supporting all of the school's programs by attending as many events and activities as possible.

The best teachers are not always at the top of the salary schedule. Likewise, the best person for any job isn't always the most expensive or the most highly credentialed. Don't pay for a certificate if you don't need one and don't want one.

Never employ nonlicensed personnel just because they are cheaper. But if they are cheaper *and better*, the choice should be obvious. Any time you can get the best for less, it's a no-brainer. It's classic fiscal fitness.

Is Outsourcing an Answer?

Occasionally, the best way to accomplish more with less is to let someone else do part of the work at a lower cost than you can do it yourself. Privatization (i.e., contracting out certain services) is a big deal now with governmental units at all levels—including schools. The attraction is reduced cost and increased management flexibility.

Is it cheaper and more efficient to farm out selected functions than to have them performed internally? For example, is it more cost-effective to have someone else provide some services, such as food service or transportation, than doing it yourself? Is the cheapest way always the best way? Sometimes, yes. Sometimes, no. Sometimes the amount saved makes privatization imperative. Sometimes, politics make it impossible. It's your job as leader to figure it out.

When outsourcing occurs in schools, it is almost always accompanied by considerable political and emotional heat. If you're not able and willing to take the heat, don't even think about privatization. (Remember Harry Truman's comment about staying in the kitchen? His advice applies to school administrators as well as to politicians.)

In most school situations, the following service areas are the most likely candidates for possible privatization:

- Custodial services
- Food service
- Student transportation
- Public relations
- Security
- Application screening
- Technology installation and repair
- Psychological testing and other psychological services
- Low-incident special education services

When weighing the pros and cons of outsourcing, it may be helpful to remember that it's your responsibility to spend money wisely to help kids, not to help current or wannabe employees.

If you do make the decision to privatize certain functions, preparation is the best approach. Allow plenty of lead time and honor all current contract provisions. In addition, these strategies can help affected staff members accept and cope with the change:

1. Tell the truth—including the worst-case scenario.
2. Share priorities (reasons).
3. Be sensitive to feelings. (Lead with your heart; follow with your head.)
4. Make every effort to be generous with severance provisions and reasonable continuation of health benefits for personnel laid off due to outsourcing.
5. Do what you can to get the new vendor or provider to employ your displaced personnel.
6. Provide other outplacement counseling and other services as needed.

Outsourcing isn't always popular. But finding more money to spend on kids is. Don't back away from privatization just because it's uncomfortable or unwelcome by some factions.

Outsourcing can be viewed as just another dimension of getting more out of staff for less. But in this case, it's someone else's staff. If you're looking for guidance as to when to privatize and when not to, try common sense. It still works.

Volunteers: How to Get Them, Use Them, and Keep Them Coming Back

If you really want to get more done in your school with the same or less staff, the best advice is to use all the free help you can get. Volunteers are the life's blood of today's most effective schools. If schools have unsung heroes, they are the parents and other community members who help out without pay.

Unfortunately, some teachers and administrators are still suspicious of volunteers. They don't want other adults in the classroom. They fear intrusion or interference, even, perhaps, discovery. They're afraid of the wrong thing. They should fear blowing an opportunity to get all children all the help and attention they need.

Good schools can't do business without volunteers today. That's why the best leaders welcome all the volunteer help they can get and ask for more. You should, too.

If you are serious about fiscal fitness, become a fanatic about bringing no-cost extra help into the school. Act like you invented volunteerism. You'll be glad you did. And so will your students.

Example: Volunteer Coordinator's Job Description

Responsibilities

1. Plan and implement volunteer service programs that make full use of available human and physical resources.
2. Establish volunteer policies and guidelines.
3. Recruit, train, and evaluate volunteers.
4. Evaluate program effectiveness.
5. Develop a strong liaison among volunteers, staff, and administration regarding volunteer services.
6. Evaluate staff volunteer needs and develop and implement programs that meet those needs.
7. Ensure community and staff involvement by establishing a volunteer advisory council.
8. Organize and implement appreciation and recognition functions for volunteers, including districtwide recognition events and personal growth workshops.
9. Maintain necessary records, files, and time sheets for all volunteers.
10. Provide training for regular staff on effective use and management of volunteers.
11. Develop and monitor business-education partnerships.
12. Serve as liaison to state and national volunteer organizations.

The best way to start is to view everyone as a potential volunteer. Volunteers come in all sizes and shapes. They can be parents, business representatives, retirees, grandparents, students, or other community members.

Constantly look for new ways to connect kids and adults in learning situations. If not enough volunteers come to you, go to them. Don't be too proud to recruit.

Following are some of the ways volunteer-rich schools go about enlisting donations of time and talent:

- Link up with city government to hire a shared volunteer coordinator (see Job Description above). A full-time coordinator can quickly pay for his or her salary by promoting volunteerism (bringing more volunteers into the school or city hall) and matching up willing helpers with tasks that need to be done.

- Make signing up to volunteer a routine part of back-to-school parent meetings and open houses. Don't ask parents if they want to volunteer. Ask them which volunteer activity they choose to engage in. Convince them that volunteering, like monitoring homework, is part of the deal.

- When recruiting, avoid overusing the term *volunteer*. For some people, it evokes a negative stereotype. It works better to use titles for specific volunteer functions, such as tutor, library assistant, or director of first impressions (for a receptionist).

- Use catch phrases such as "get involved," "become part of," or simply "help."

- Adopt slogans that generate interest such as "Each time you share yourself with another, two people grow."

- Use quotations and testimonials that appeal to people's higher instincts such as,

> *"Volunteering in the schools is one way to help young people and provide them with connections to other caring adults."*
>
> —Karen Davidman, Volunteer Coordinator

- Encourage organizations (service clubs, businesses, etc.) to have members volunteer as a group. It makes volunteering more comfortable and more fun.

- Use an application form for volunteers, something like Form 2.1. It makes volunteering seem more important, business-like, and professional. Written applications make it easier to match interests and needs. They also help sort out undesirable candidates.

One caution should be noted about recruiting volunteers. Although you want as many volunteers as you can get, you don't want everyone. In today's society, there are a lot of predators and other misguided individuals who can pose a threat to children. Don't let it happen on your watch.

In the interest of child safety, limited liability, and risk management, responsible school officials must be absolutely meticulous

FORM 2.1 Sample Volunteer Program Application Form

Volunteer Program Application Form

Date: _____

Name: _____   Home phone: _____

Work phone: _____   Fax # _____

Home address: _____

_____

Business address: _____

_____

Volunteer Interests (You may check more than one):

___ Mentor   ___ Tutor   ___ ESL   ___ Grandparent   ___ Classroom

___ Helper   ___ Art Appreciation   ___ Media Center   ___ Book Nook

___ Resource Speaker   ___ Other

Education/work experience: _____

_____

_____

Special hobbies/skills: _____

_____

_____

Why do you want to volunteer? _____

_____

_____

Preferred school: _____

Preferred grade level(s): _____

continued

Ramsey, R. *Fiscal Fitness for School Administrators.* ©2001. Corwin Press, Inc.

FORM 2.1 Continued

Availability:

Days   *Time(s)*

___ Mon.   ___ a.m.   ___ p.m.   ___ hours per week

___ Tues.   ___ a.m.   ___ p.m.   ___ once per month

___ Wed.   ___ a.m.   ___ p.m.   ___ occasionally

___ Thurs.   ___ a.m.   ___ p.m.   ___ once

___ Fri.   ___ a.m.   ___ p.m.   ___ other

Entire year _____   3 months _____   6 months _____

List any special knowledge or skills that you would like to share as a classroom resource speaker: _____

_____

_____

Could you help on short-term projects such as vision screening, phone surveys, and so on? _____

_____

_____

Have you ever been convicted of a felony? _____

List two references:

Name _____   Name _____

Phone _____   Phone _____

Address _____   Address _____

Relationship _____   Relationship_____

Signature _____   Date _____

Note: A background check may be conducted as a safety measure for children.

Ramsey, R. *Fiscal Fitness for School Administrators.* ©2001. Corwin Press, Inc.

Volunteer Opportunities in Schools (a partial list)

Media center helper
Room parent
Art appreciation volunteer
Minicourses teacher
Tutor
PTA board member
One-to-one volunteer
Driver
Classroom helper
Club advisor
Book Nook reader
Stage manager
Resource speaker
Computer aide
Music appreciation volunteer
Equipment manager
English as a second language
Greeter
Vocabulary builder
Costume designer
Grandparent volunteer
Choreographer
Mentor
Accompanist
Bus rider
Debate judge
Preschool screener
Party organizer
Career resource person
Get-out-the-vote person
Junior Great Books discussion

Volunteer leader
Landscape helper
Crossing guard
Playground aide
Library assistant
Fundraising volunteer
Ticket taker
Block home parent
Community reader
Big brother or big sister
Musician (to play along with
    orchestra/band students)
Office aide
Sports official
Gymnastics spotter
Test timer
Chaperone
Sports team scout
Piano tuner
Usher
Bus stop monitor
Prompter
Theme reader
Storyteller
Caller
Artist-in-residence
Advisory council member
Binder Buddy[a]
Interpreter
Field trip helper

—Whew!

a. Some schools provide each student with a Franklin Planner and assign volunteers
   to check periodically and help students use them to their full advantage.

about running background checks on all prospective volunteers who may have one-on-one contact with children (including with teenagers). Anything less is malpractice.

Once recruited, the next step is to make full and effective use of every volunteer. There's nothing worse than having an eager volunteer present, ready, and willing to work, and no one knows what to do with him or her.

Most schools have only scratched the surface in tapping the full scope of volunteer potential. Their use is limited only by the staff's inability to perceive all the possibilities. Countless functions that must be carried out in the daily operation of the school (see previous list) can be performed as well by a qualified volunteer who is properly trained and supervised as by a paid staff member. Of course, some tasks cannot be performed by volunteers, such as disciplining students and providing security in high-risk areas.

Whatever capacity volunteers are assigned to, it pays to have predetermined guidelines that are agreed upon by both regular staff members and volunteer personnel (see sample guidelines below).

The final secret to a successful volunteer program is to keep good people coming back. Whether volunteers return again and again de-

Sample: Guidelines for Volunteers

- *Dependability:* Please be dependable. The teachers and students are counting on you.
- *Communication:* If you have questions or comments, communicate with the coordinator, teacher, or principal. NO question is inappropriate.
- *Support:* Volunteers are requested by teachers or principals. The volunteer functions strictly in a supportive role.
- *Confidentiality:* Respect the confidentiality of your relationship to the school. Your knowledge of students is a privileged communication to be shared only with responsible staff members.
- *Discipline:* Discipline is the responsibility of the classroom teacher or principal. The school policy on discipline is available in the office.
- *Contact With Students:* Volunteers' contact with students is limited to their scheduled times.

pends on whether they are *successful* and *appreciated*. As an administrator, it's your job to see that this happens.

Never take volunteers for granted. Pamper them. It pays. The following perks will go a long way toward building volunteer loyalty and satisfaction.

- Provide targeted training for all volunteers. It will help them do a better job and feel better about it.
- Give all volunteers an easily recognizable name tag. It will affect how they are perceived and treated by the regular staff.
- Reserve VIP parking spots for volunteers. Everyone appreciates this type of special treatment.
- Provide day care. It makes volunteering accessible to many more people. There's no reason you can't have a volunteer to provide day care for other volunteers.
- Use the RAVE approach to working with volunteers: **R**espect, **A**ppreciation, **V**alidation, and **E**ncouragement.
- Find creative ways to recognize all volunteers (see examples below).

Ten Ways to Recognize Volunteers

1. Create a Wall of Fame with pictures and bios of regular volunteers.
2. Issue personalized coffee mugs to volunteers.
3. Let volunteers go to the front of the cafeteria line.
4. Issue "We ♥ Volunteers" T-shirts or sweatshirts.
5. Celebrate volunteers' birthdays.
6. Give each volunteer an appreciation card signed by the students.
7. Give volunteers free passes to school events (games, plays, concerts).
8. Dedicate an assembly program or instrumental concert to a special volunteer.
9. Hold a special year-end party to celebrate volunteers.
10. Give successful volunteers first consideration for job openings.

The final word on volunteers is that you haven't done enough until you've saturated the school with competent, caring adults who are excited about helping kids. That's the kind of school you would want for your child. Why not make it happen for all children?

It doesn't cost any more to have 50 volunteers in your school than it does to have none. No responsible educator can pass up a bargain like that.

Get Better Administration With Less Money

You may not think your school spends too much on administration; but everyone else does. They may be right.

If you want to become a hero in the eyes of the teacher unions, parents, taxpayers, and the school board, all you have to do is find ways to redirect dollars from administrative functions back to the classroom. Sound impossible? It's not.

Most schools could get better administration at less cost. But they don't. What's usually lacking isn't the knowledge or creativity to streamline school administration, but the will to do it.

The trick to getting more for less in administration is to stretch leadership by widening the span of control or broadening responsibilities and being willing to make some tough trade-offs. The quickest and easiest ways to start are to replace high-salaried administrators with unpaid or low-paid administrative interns and/or to let site councils (volunteer parents) assume some management functions.

One of the best examples of improving administrative efficiency and effectiveness while holding the line on costs can be found at St. Louis Park (Minnesota) Junior High School, where principal Les Bork has used trade-offs to give better service and save money at the same time. Bork has traded off one assistant principal, two counselors, and a half-time social worker for four deans (see the box on p. 47).

The new model reduces redundancy, clarifies roles, and increases access to administration for both students and parents. It focuses more on the child and less on separate and discrete functions such as counseling or management.

Under the new plan, each administrator (dean) serves fewer students. Parents like it because they have only one person to call no matter what kind of problem their child has (academic, social, or discipline). Bork calls it a one-stop shopping approach.

The role of the deans at St. Louis Park is to facilitate the overall academic achievement and social development of each student. They function as generalists, not specialists. Cost savings occur because the deans are paid on the teachers' salary schedule, rather than administrators' wages. Consequently, the four deans cost the same (or sometimes even less) as previously was spent on three and a half specialists (an administrator, two counselors, and a half-time social worker).

Administrative Efficiency Model for St. Louis Park (MN) Jr. High School

Traditional Model	*New Model*
1. Adminstration Staffing: 1 principal 1 assistant principal (AP) 2 counselors ½ social worker	1. Administration Staffing: 1 principal 4 deans
2. Access: • AP sole disciplinarian for 750 students • Each counselor serves 350 students • Social worker serves all families	2. Access: • Each dean serves only 150 students
3. Disadvantages: • *Confusion.* Parents didn't know who to call • *Redundancy.* Both the AP and a counselor had to sign off on schedule changes, educational plans, and so on. • *Gaps in Service.* If AP absent, discipline came to a standstill.	3. Advantages: • *Better Access.* Parents and students have only one administrative contact. • *Greater Efficiency.* One administrator is responsible for all aspects of the student's development. • *Continuity.* If one dean is absent, others can cover without any interruption of service.

The St. Louis Park model isn't perfect; but it represents a start toward getting more for less. Any beginning is a good beginning. What trade-offs can you make to provide better administration for less money? Why don't you make them?

In every employee category in your school, there are economies, efficiencies, and savings waiting to happen. Whether it's through reallocation—by greater reliance on interns, part-time help, non-licensed personnel, or volunteers, by privatization, by getting more out of existing staff, by the broadening of administrative responsibilities—or through some other means, there are numerous ways to accomplish as much or more with less staff. But cost savings won't happen by themselves.

No one is going to ask to be first in line to get cut, privatized, stretched, or reallocated. You have to look for the opportunities.

Cost-effectiveness is a choice. As leader, you get to do the choosing. It's not always fun; but it is your job. Just do it!

3

How to Get the Biggest Bang for Your Program Buck

Conditioning is good for individuals. Why not for organizations? Shedding excess weight, replacing fat with muscle, firming up soft spots, and becoming leaner, trimmer, and firmer makes people stronger and healthier. It can work that way for schools as well. Stretching program dollars is a form of conditioning that can create a better school.

Of course, it's no secret that most of us don't like the discipline and rigor of conditioning. It's hard work to get and stay in shape. It often takes a personal trainer to keep us on track. Likewise, schools sometimes need a kind of personal trainer to help them achieve optimum fiscal fitness. That's what administrators are for.

Naturally, educators don't like to ration resources, effect efficiencies, or cut back on programs. The greatest obstacles to tightening up school programs are almost always the vested interests of those who developed the program in the first place, the persistence of history and habit, and plain old-fashioned resistance to change. The good news is that obstacles exist to be overcome.

Program reduction isn't necessarily bad. There's a difference between stripping and streamlining school programs. When resources are finite, programs have to be trimmed or reshaped occasionally to make them more focused and defensible. Reducing or redefining programs then becomes an exercise in conditioning that can result in a trimmer, better, healthier school.

In good times or bad, effective school leaders continuously strive to realize higher-than-expected results at lower-than-expected costs. Stretching existing resources and getting the biggest bang for the school's investment may mean reducing some programs of limited benefit in order to preserve the health of the overall organization. The trick is in understanding the trade-offs.

Fortunately, there are certain school-tested criteria and guidelines that can help you make better belt-tightening program decisions and make your school even stronger and more vibrant in the process.

Cut the Fat Without Cutting the Muscle

Every program or service is indispensable and untouchable to someone. The truth, however, is that every curricular, extracurricular, or other school program can be operated more economically, efficiently, and effectively than it is today. If you don't believe this is true in your school, you don't know what's going on, you're in a state of denial, or you're missing the point of fiscal fitness. Look around. The best administrators you know are constantly looking for (and finding) ways to do things better with fewer resources.

Getting more for your money is never a bad idea. Innovation isn't always about spending more, expanding, or adding on. Sometimes the most creative thing a school staff can do is to consolidate, contract, compact, reduce, redesign, or realign existing programs rather than generating new ones. If more staffs were to adopt this premise, schools would be able to free up significant resources for use wherever they are most needed.

Periodically, every school program, from food service and transportation to athletics and reading, should be scrutinized for possible efficiencies and savings. Sooner or later, many will need radical surgery, some paring back, or at the very least a little liposuction. Of course, this won't happen unless someone with authority requires it. As the administrator-in-charge, that's your job. It's called leadership.

In horticulture, thinning and weeding are positive measures. In forestry, the healthiest trees can be made even stronger with proper pruning. These same principles can apply to programs in schools.

Is it possible to cut the fat out of school programs without cutting the muscle? You bet. It starts by setting clear-cut, no-nonsense priorities.

For example, when considering possible reductions or economies in instructional programs, many successful schools rank existing offerings in priority order using the four-tier model.

Four-Tier Program Ranking

1. Programs *mandated* by law or regulation
2. *Core* programs (i.e., graduation requirements)
3. Schedule *commitments* (e.g., fourth- or fifth-year foreign language)
4. *Optional* programs (usually high-cost, low-enrollment programs or those that overlap or duplicate other offerings)

A more down-to-earth version, which parents and community members may prefer, simply sorts programs into the following easy-to-understand categories: Carved in Stone, Sacred Cows, Hometown Favorites, and Icing on the Cake.

No matter what model is used, categorizing programs helps define limits (what's out of bounds) and pinpoint possibilities (what's fair game).

Once program priorities have been established, the real work can begin. Gathering data and evidence on program effectiveness is essential to sound decision making regarding possible economies or cutbacks.

Most veteran administrators use some combination of the following sources for gaining insights into what is and is not working in existing programs:

- Test results
- Follow-up studies
- Consumer surveys
- Classroom observations
- Exit interviews
- Student work and portfolios
- Formal research studies (experimental and control groups)
- Feedback from consultants (friendly critics)

Depending on the nature, scope, and severity of action under consideration, parent and community input and involvement may also be necessary or desirable (see the example on the next page).

It's a mistake, however, to determine program reductions by plebiscite or opinion poll. Professionals are held accountable for educational results. The people on the street, who are merely expressing an opinion, are not. Decisions about which programs will stay and which will go should be based on more than a Nielson-like rating system.

Example: Simplifying Citizen Input

In 1996, the Forest Grove (Oregon) School District, (503) 359-2419, received the Magna Award for providing meaningful community participation in setting priorities for budget reductions.

Committed to using real numbers and ordinary citizens rather than relying on a panel of experts, the district boiled down its complicated, multifaceted budget to a single page. Citizens were then asked to make their recommendations for cutting $6 out of a micro-budget totaling $100.

Who says school budget makers can't be creative?

When all the pertinent data have been gathered, it's decision time. Making program reductions and alterations involves tough decisions; but that's no excuse for not making them. If they were easy to make, there wouldn't be much need for principals, supervisors, and other administrators.

You can streamline programs, stretch resources, and still retain quality if you are willing to take chances, make choices, rise above the paralysis of politics, and take the heat from obstructionists and naysayers. If you're not up to these challenges, you're not ready for fiscal fitness anyway.

Fortunately, help is available. The following criteria and guidelines have aided many schools in determining how to cut out program fat without cutting any muscle. These same pointers can help you and your staff as well.

Guiding Principles for Realizing Program Savings

1. Start by rejecting the notion that "more is better." This is conventional wisdom that is no longer conventional or wise.

2. Never cut just for cutting's sake. Have a reason.

3. Don't play games by making cosmetic or phony cuts. Be sure that every reduction really saves one dollar for every dollar cut.

4. Don't automatically reduce or eliminate any program just because only a few students are affected. The program may be the only way to provide critical experiences for these particular kids.

5. Never assume that today's most popular programs will continue to be popular or relevant tomorrow. (Whatever happened to typing classes?)

6. Look twice at any programs that don't directly contribute to fulfilling the school's mission and goals.

7. Separate programs from personalities. A marginal program taught by a charismatic teacher may appear more important and necessary than it really is.

8. Keep in mind that kids know what programs they like, but they don't always know what they need.

9. Don't retain programs for sentimental reasons. If a program has outlived its usefulness, update it or dump it.

10. If a program isn't producing the desired results, find out why before writing it off. It may only need adjusting, not eliminating. Always look for what should be salvaged as well as what should be scrapped.

11. Your goal should always be to make cocurricular programs as self-supporting as possible.

12. Trim support programs before reducing core programs.

13. When possible, reduce senior high and middle school programs before cutting elementary school programs.

14. Ask the following tough questions about every program under review:

    a. Do we need this program? Why?

    b. Do we need it in its present form?

    c. Does it need this much time?

    d. Do we need to spend this much money on it?

    e. Does it require this much staff?

     f. Does it stand alone? Can it be combined or consolidated with other programs?

     g. Is it duplicated somewhere else (in or out of the school)?

     h. Does it fit with the school's mission, goals, and strategic plan?

     i. Is this the best we can do or can we do the same thing better, more efficiently? How?

     j. What if we were to eliminate it?

15. Try to avoid eliminating any program. It's always difficult to reinstate a program once it has been completely wiped out.

These pointers can help guide decision making about economies in any kind of school program; but they are particularly useful in finding ways to get the most out of the school's curriculum investment.

If you can identify means for operating a more efficient transportation or food service program, the school board will think you are a smart administrator. But if you can figure out how to provide the same quality of curriculum at reduced costs, they'll think you are a genius. It may not be as difficult as you think.

Stretching Curriculum Dollars

Educators often joke that "it's easier to move a cemetery than it is to change the curriculum." This may be an exaggeration, but it seems true when you're trying to maintain a quality program of instruction while conserving resources. Stretching curriculum dollars is always difficult; but that doesn't make it impossible.

Part of the problem is that too many teachers and administrators still think that the best curriculum is the most comprehensive and the fastest growing. They're wrong.

A sound curriculum today needs to be well defined, focused, and sequenced. It doesn't have to be expansive or expensive.

A bloated curriculum does the students, the school, and the community no favors. This is a lesson that many school leaders learned in the 1960s and 1970s. During the bonanza days of federally funded educational development and innovation, as part of Lyndon Johnson's "Great Society," school curriculums exploded. Course offerings proliferated everywhere. Most urban high schools began offering literally hundreds of separate subjects and courses.

The result was fragmented and fractured learning—not better education. The lesson of the Great Society should be relearned for the new millennium. It's a matter of fiscal fitness.

The best way to manage curriculum costs is to let the curriculum drive the budget. Too often, the opposite is true. When the budget comes first and propels the curriculum, the instructional program takes a roller coaster ride. When the school economy is good, the curriculum flourishes. When funds for education are scarce, the curriculum shrinks. A more evenhanded approach makes more sense.

Under curriculum-driven budgeting, money is allocated first to where it is needed most as far as it will go. Such a budget is less influenced by the bias or whims of individual educators or powerful school board members.

In order for curriculum to truly drive the budget, the program of instruction must be broken down into distinct increments or pieces (building blocks) that are carefully prioritized. As Dr. William K. Poston, professor of educational administration at Iowa State University, explains, "Programs must be broken into packages or increments, costed separately, rank-ordered in preference, and funded in ordinal fashion up to the limit of available resources."

This approach allows the school staff to reclaim control and make the most of every curriculum dollar. Curriculum-driven budgeting works best when the budget process is public and participatory. This openness promotes teamwork, acceptance, and commitment.

Some administrators are afraid to embrace this method of budgeting because they think they then have to become experts in all facets of the curriculum. They don't.

All they really need to manage this process efficiently and effectively is an understanding of what makes a good curriculum. Following are the basics most educators agree on:

- No curriculum should be ethereal or mysterious. It should be made up of down-to-earth stuff that students need to learn, know, and do to succeed on a daily basis.

- The best curriculum is a balanced curriculum.

- The curriculum is for all learners. You don't need a completely different curriculum for every different ability level.

- There should be an academic core of content that provides focus and cohesion to the overall curriculum.

- The curriculum should be flexible enough to allow for unique "teachable moments."

- The curriculum should be focused on what kids need to learn, not just what educators want to teach.

- The curriculum should be inclusive, unbiased, and globally oriented.

- A good curriculum is future focused.

- The Information Age requires a curriculum that is resource-based, not bound to textbooks.

- Teaching process to students is usually more important than teaching specific content to them.

- The curriculum should be as interdisciplinary as possible.

- The curriculum should reach beyond the classroom.

- Somewhere in the curriculum, every student should have opportunities to "post hole"[1] for depth.

- The curriculum can only be stretched so far. When new content, subjects, or topics are added, something else has to go.

- The curriculum is only as good as the staff development program that supports it.

- The curriculum doesn't have to be bland, antiseptic, or value free.

- The curriculum can be fun. There is joy in learning, and it should show.

Armed with these understandings, it's easier for any administrator to channel resources where they are needed most.

There are a lot of ways besides adopting a curriculum-driven budget to stretch program dollars without jeopardizing the integrity or quality of the instructional program. Following are some starter suggestions to consider:

1. Institute a program of "curriculum mapping" to determine if what you say you are teaching is actually being taught. You may be surprised by how many extraneous topics are creeping into the curriculum and crowding out the intended content.

2. Stop "social promotions." They cheat students, scam parents, and increase costs in the long run. Insist that students master material early on and avoid remedial costs later.

3. Offer low-enrollment courses on alternate years. This maintains availability of the courses to all interested students at a fraction of the cost.

4. Identify those content areas and skills that can be taught just as well or better by other agencies (e.g., driver education).

5. Use teleconferencing to share courses and teachers with other schools or districts.

6. Allow students to take more courses independently or by appointment.

7. Whenever possible, consolidate high school courses with enrollments of fewer than 12 students (e.g., combine fourth- and fifth-year French into one class).

8. Limit the number of advanced placement courses offered. Colleges put a cap on the number of advanced placement credits students can carry into college, so there is no need to offer every conceivable advanced placement program.

9. Give credit for validated community service experiences. It promotes real-world learning and doesn't require any more paid staff.

10. Maximize the use of free and low-cost instructional materials.

11. Adopt new textbooks less often and purchase good-condition used textbooks when available.

12. Eliminate duplication of content (e.g., some secondary schools teach photography in both the industrial technology department and the fine arts department).

13. Limit the number of foreign languages taught. No school can offer them all. The more limited the number of languages offered, the larger the classes. Large classes equal greater efficiency.

14. Don't teach technology as a separate subject. Make it part of every curricular area. Today, technology is the medium, not the message.

15. Minimize activities that give the most practice to those who need it the least (e.g., spelling bees).

16. Compact selected year-long courses into one-semester offerings instead.

17. Volunteer to be a pilot school to test new curriculum and instructional materials provided free by the publisher.

18. Minimize tracking. Some schools split hairs and go overboard in differentiating ability levels and creating separate tracks. The more tracks, the greater the cost. Use common sense.

19. Quit teaching public service topics such as gun safety or baby-sitting skills. Give these responsibilities back to parents and the community.

20. Arrange for your local college to offer beginning courses on your high school site so that better students can get concurrent high school and college credit for taking them. This way, the college pays for advanced courses that might otherwise come out of your school's budget.

21. Extend the cycle of curriculum review and revision (e.g, from every 5 years to every 6 years).

22. Use assessment to drive instruction. Teach kids what they need to learn, not what they already know.

Economies beget more economies. Simply implementing cost-saving strategies, such as those above, frequently brings additional possibilities to the surface. Streamlining the curriculum can become a self-fulfilling prophecy. Once you believe you can do it, you can—and will.

Obviously, there are savings to be found within the mainstream curriculum. It shouldn't be a great revelation that the same thing is often true of the special education program as well.

Redefine Special Education, Improve Programs, and Save Money

No one questions the value of special education; yet almost everyone questions the cost.

It doesn't take a doctorate degree in school finance to grasp that providing special programs for handicapped, disabled, and other students with unique needs is expensive. The lower the incidence of a particular disability, the higher the cost for providing an appropriate educational program.

Unfortunately for school districts, the costs keep escalating as Congress and the courts periodically expand the number and variety of special education services that must be offered (see the following partial list). Ever since the federal and state governments first began dictating special education services, without matching their mandates with the money to pay for them, school districts have been scrambling for resources to cover the costs.

Mandated Special Education Programs (a partial list)[a]

By law, public schools are currently required to provide education and other services for students with the following disorders and problems:

Early childhood health and developmental problems

Physical impairments

Vision and hearing impairments

Mental disabilities

Learning disabilities

Attention deficit disorders (ADD)

Emotional and behavioral disorders (EBD)

Communication disorders

Speech and language disorders

Occupational and physical therapy needs

a. This list is subject to change as new legislation, regulations, and court interpretations occur.

Many districts are now spending up to 19% or more of their total budget for special education programs that serve relatively small numbers of students. Some leading administrators feel that these costs are out of control and now jeopardize the overall fiscal integrity of the system. A few have become so desperate that they've explored the possibility of tapping into parents' health insurance to cover some of the costs. (Don't try it. It doesn't work, and it's not cost-effective.)

In some worst-case scenarios, the funding issue has polarized entire communities and pitted mainstream parents against special education parents. Don't let this happen on your watch. The enemy is not the regular parents, nor is it the special education parents, who only want the programs and services their children are entitled to receive. The problem lies in a flawed system.

Obviously, it costs more to educate pupils with special needs than the rest of the population, just as it costs more to maintain a football team than a swim team. It doesn't matter. It's the school's responsibility to do it all. School leaders have to find ways to avoid rifts between community factions and to get all parents to work together to secure adequate funding for all programs.

The answer, of course, is for government to own up to its responsibility for fully funding whatever programs it mandates. Realistically and politically, however, this isn't going to happen any time soon. In the meantime, the best an administrator can do is to control costs as much as possible and seek creative ways to provide special education services more efficiently and effectively.

Fortunately, school officials are not helpless in dealing with the problem. Fiscal fitness truly is for everyone—even special education advocates. There are workable ways to restrain, even reduce, costs and still deliver essential programs to the students who need them. Following are the four keys to cost containment in special education:

1. Know and follow the letter of the law.
2. Invest in early interventions and safety nets.
3. Adopt a realistic definition of eligibility for services.
4. Serve as many special education students as possible within your own school or district.

The first secret to successfully managing special education expenses is to keep current on relevant legislation and litigation, do what the law says you have to do (but don't exceed mandates unless you have ample resources to do so), and stay out of court as much as possible.

It pays to hire competent legal counsel with experience and expertise in special education case law and to follow the advice you pay for. It doesn't pay to try to cut corners or duck any of your responsibilities under the law.

If you faithfully fulfill your legal and moral obligations and are willing to use mediation or other reasonable means to settle disputes, you can avoid many potentially costly court battles. In the case of an extreme situation, however, one in which parental demands and expectations are outrageous, dare to go to court to prove you're right. The savings can be substantial.

The stakes are high in special education. Bad precedent and sloppy practice can be ruinous in the long run. That's why effective school leaders insist on meticulous record keeping, attention to detail, and careful listening to what special needs parents and students are saying. Doing the right things right the first time every time is always a good way to save money.

The second step in cost containment for special education programs is to spend money early on to avoid spending a lot more later. Prevention and prudence go together.

By investing in early intervention programs and safety nets (see examples on p. 62), your school can nip many problems in the bud and catch many struggling students before their problems require more costly remediation.

The best (and cheapest) time to solve problems is now. Delay costs money. This is particularly true when many safety net programs rely on aides and volunteers, whereas formal special education and other remedial programs require high-priced professionals and specialists. When it comes to prioritized spending, put all the money you can into early intervention. As retailers constantly remind us, "Spend now and save."

The third (and perhaps most effective) approach to controlling special education costs is to tighten up eligibility requirements so that they realistically reflect the incidence of disability among the student population. As administrator, you have some control in defining who's eligible for special education services and who's not. Don't squander a single opportunity to sharpen the definition of eligibility or you're bound to incur greater future costs by default.

Not every child who is inattentive, fidgety, or rebellious has an attention deficit disorder (ADD) or an emotional and behavioral disorder (EBD). Some are simply spoiled, lazy, unmotivated, or starved for attention and affection. These are problems that do not require expensive special education solutions.

Many existing eligibility standards are vague and wide open to varied interpretation—especially those that don't always require a

Examples: Instructional Safety Nets of Naranco Elementary School, El Cajon, CA[a]

ABCs tutoring	Healthy Start
Student success teams	Reading Recovery
Reading folders	Study skills support
Reading Is Fun Club	After-school reading groups
Special Friends (mentors)	ELI (early literacy intervention)
English Is Fun Club	Student support groups
PIP (primary intervention program)	Rotary reading
	P.A.T. (Parents as Teachers)
Discovery Club	Rolling Reading tutors (literacy volunteers)
Homework Club	
Peer mediators	AL (accelerated literacy)

a. Safety nets and interventions that are designed to help head off special education costs

medical diagnosis, such as emotional and behavioral problems. This makes it easy for some marginal teachers to use the ill-defined EBD classification as a means for removing disruptive students from their classrooms. This defeats the purpose. There are better and cheaper discipline measures than misusing special education referrals.

Even when a medical diagnosis is required, mistakes can be made. If school personnel question a specific diagnosis, they shouldn't hesitate to request a second opinion. Parents do it all the time.

When redefining special education to clarify who really belongs and who doesn't, the goal isn't to push deserving students out of the program, but to make the system more efficient and accountable. This is what fiscal fitness is all about.

The final key to conserving resources is to serve special education students in-house whenever possible. Contracting with outside agencies to deliver programs and services for students with disabilities is expensive. Some say extravagant. (Transportation alone can be a big ticket item.)

More and more schools and districts are finding that they can save money and even improve the quality of some special education programs by providing more of these services on their own.

For the 1999-2000 school year, the Minnetonka (Minnesota) School District projected savings of approximately $100,000 merely by shifting some special education programs away from outside providers. Providing special-needs students with programs and services closer to home promotes greater consistency and encourages stronger student-staff relationships. That's why in Minnetonka and elsewhere, keeping special education students at home is proving to be a win-win situation for everyone.

You can't transform a high-priced special education program into a low-cost operation; you can reign in costs by making programs more efficient and productive. If you don't, you'll wish you had.

Avoid Short-Changing Gifted Students
Even During Periods of Retrenchment

Programs for gifted and talented students don't have the same legal and emotional backing that services for disabled students enjoy. Nevertheless, gifted kids deserve to be supported, stretched, and challenged commensurate with their ability just as all students do. This can get expensive. But it doesn't have to.

It doesn't necessarily take high-priced special teachers or costly pull-out programs to provide gifted students with what they need to succeed and reach their full potential. Most educators now agree on the basic goals for gifted education. Fortunately, none of these require excessive amounts of extra funding.

The list of goals is doable for any school or district regardless of wealth. The best programs for achieving goals aren't automatically the most costly. It doesn't always take more money to educate gifted students properly. Sometimes it just takes understanding, commitment, passion, and the right attitude.

Naturally, it would be irresponsible not to spend enough money to meet the needs of your best and brightest students. Likewise, it would be irresponsible to spend a lot more than it takes to do the job while short-changing other important areas in the process. Effective administrators do neither.

Goals for Gifted Education

- Identify pupils who are intellectually gifted.
- Understand the abilities, needs, and interests of individual gifted and talented students.
- Help gifted students gain a realistic and healthy self-concept.
- Help gifted students become self-actualized, self-disciplined, and self-motivated.
- Prepare gifted students for productive roles in society.
- Help gifted children grow into creative, productive, and compassionate adults.
- Help gifted students appreciate and respect individual differences.
- Foster higher-level thinking skills in all gifted students.
- Help gifted students nurture their leadership skills and acquire other skills for the future.

It is possible to spend only a reasonable amount on programs for gifted students and still get unreasonably good results, even during periods of retrenchment.

Following are a dozen low-cost and no-cost strategies that many successful schools have used and are using to meet the needs of gifted children and youth:

1. Dare to accelerate. Allowing students to skip grades and move ahead in school has fallen into disfavor in some communities. It's too bad, because acceleration works. When social maturity and development match intellectual ability, acceleration is still one of the best ways to accommodate exceptional students. Best of all, it's basically free.

2. Implement an Early Entrance program so that advanced children can start school early and get a jump start on their education. This is just another form of low-cost acceleration.

3. Cluster two to four gifted students together in a class. One gifted student in a class can become bored and isolated. Several exceptional students together, however, continually

challenge and motivate each other. They also serve as good role models for the rest of the class.

4. Hire an advocate who works for and with all gifted students, rather than a special teacher who can work only with a few (see Job Description example on p. 66).

5. Teach higher-level thinking skills to all students (see Bloom's Taxonomy on p. 67). It is no longer necessary to pull out gifted students to teach them these skills. We now know that all pupils can benefit from instruction in higher-level thinking. This illustrates again that when we strengthen the instructional program for all students, gifted and talented kids benefit as much as or more than most.

6. Establish a MENSA mentors program by matching up adult MENSA member volunteers with gifted students for the purpose of mentoring, tutoring, mutual learning, companionship, and fun.

7. Train all teachers in how to differentiate instruction to meet the needs of all ability levels.

8. Arrange for gifted students to participate in creative problem-solving team competitions, such as Quiz Bowl, Math Olympiad, or DestiNation Imagination. For the small price of an advisor's stipend, you can realize a big payoff for a large number of gifted kids.

9. Band together with other schools to sponsor summer enrichment programs and camp experiences for gifted students. Local businesses are often interested in underwriting such activities.

10. Initiate a Senior Project program for gifted 12th graders. Such a program encourages exceptional students to synthesize their past learning into a personalized, independent research project that is presented to appropriate faculty members. Some schools call this a "rite of passage experience." This approach adds a new dimension to the student's learning experience without adding any staff.

11. Solicit volunteers to lead cocurricular activities for gifted students, such as Junior Great Books and Inventor's Fairs.

12. Arrange to place gifted students in leadership positions on important city and school committees and commissions

(Community Education Advisory Committee, Parks and Recreation Commission, Bike and Hike Trail Task Force, etc.).

Job Description: Advocate for Gifted and Talented Students

Responsibilities:

1. Champion the cause of gifted education within the school and the community.
2. Serve as a liaison and ombudsman for gifted students with the rest of the staff. Assist gifted pupils and their parents with school-related problems.
3. Monitor the curricular, extracurricular, and social development of gifted students in the school and maintain a portfolio of each pupil's progress and accomplishments.
4. Assist gifted students with registration, enrollment, course selection, college selection, and admission procedures.
5. Provide students and parents with information about activities, events, and opportunities for gifted students at the local, state, regional, and national levels.
6. Conduct student and/or parent "growing up gifted" discussions or support groups as needed.
7. Provide students and parents with information on post-high school planning, career choices, college selection, and financial aid resources. Assist with preparation of college applications as needed.
8. Serve as a resource for students and parents. Advise families and provide individual and group counseling in the areas of gifted education, vocational guidance, and emotional development as needed.
9. Promote development programs on teaching gifted students for the regular teaching staff.
10. Participate in local, state, regional, and national organizations for gifted education.
11. Perform other duties as assigned.

Bloom's Taxonomy of Higher-Level Thinking Skills (cognitive development)

I. Knowledge level: Recall, recognize, and retain
II. Comprehension level: Translate and interpret
III. Application level: Use in new context
IV. Analysis level: Break down and see implications
V. Synthesis level: Integrate in new ways
VI. Evaluation level: Judge information

All of these strategies are school tested and budget friendly. They exemplify fiscal fitness and the effective use of resources. Best of all, they work without bankrupting the school.

After looking at these approaches, you can probably think of many more ways to deliver efficient, effective, and economical gifted education in your school. If not, just ask your gifted and talented students to do it for you. It's another way to challenge them. And it's free.

How to Run a Low-Cost, No-Frills Activity Program That Works

Many educators call the activity program the school's "second curriculum." Activities keep many kids in school and instill some survival lessons that can't be easily taught elsewhere. Activities are morale boosters. They spark school pride and rally communities around the school. The activity program is important. Period. It isn't the school's primary mission. Activities should be responsive to fiscal realities just like every other school program.

It's no secret that some schools go overboard on athletics or other activities. We all know schools that have spent huge sums to build a sports dynasty, field a bowl-bound marching band, or erect a Taj Mahal-like edifice to showcase their sporting events.

If money is plentiful, these may be justifiable (or, at least, harmless) expenses. If money is tight, they are irresponsible extravagances. In either case, such expenditures are unnecessary.

A Representative List of Student Activities

National Honor Society

Orchestra

Caring Youth club

Quiz Bowl

AFDA (Athletes for Drug Awareness)

SADD (Students Against Drunk Driving)

Bowling club

Science Olympiad Team

Chess club

SOS (Save Our Surroundings)

Choral music

Concert band

Speech

Jazz lab

Student council

Conflict resolution mediators

Theater

Soccer

Debate

Synchronized swimming

Distributive Education Clubs of America

Gymnastics

Student newspaper

Nordic ski team

Student yearbook

Cross-country ski team

HEART (Home Economics and Related Training)

Swimming

Track team

Human Mosaic club (diversity organization)

Golf

Basketball

Literary magazine

Football

Math team

Hockey

Peer counselors

Softball

Tennis

Volleyball

The number of activities offered in American schools is staggering (see the representative list above). Any activity that a teacher, coach, parent, or student has ever thought of is offered by some school somewhere. Fortunately for budget makers, no school needs to offer them all. In fact, many schools probably offer too many. When the list of school activities is longer than the list of course offerings, you can be pretty sure that the tail is wagging the dog.

All that's really necessary to operate a no-frills activity program that works is simply to provide enough activities to meet the following goals:

- Develop interests and provide alternative uses of discretionary time.
- Promote a positive attitude toward self and others.
- Develop new skills.
- Promote physical and mental fitness.
- Instill a sense of fair play and good sportsmanship.
- Develop leadership.
- Foster commitment.
- Provide opportunities for socializing and making new friends.
- Have fun.
- Experience success.
- Enhance involvement in the school.

None of these goals says anything about winning championships, marching at bowl games, wearing expensive uniforms, or spending more on athletic facilities than on libraries and science labs. Schools don't have to spend more, win more, or offer more to have a viable activity program. You'll know that your program is enough when it meets the following criteria. Nothing more. Nothing less.

Earmarks of an Effective Activity Program

An effective activity program

1. Is fluid (adjusts to flow of student interests and needs)
2. Involves real learning
3. Is accessible and affordable
4. Stresses cooperation as well as competition
5. Includes equal opportunities for both sexes (see the guidelines on the next page)
6. Eliminates elitism and strives to involve uninvolved students
7. Maximizes participation
8. Recognizes cultural differences
9. Provides adapted activities for students with disabilities
10. Features qualified coaches and advisors
11. Uses community resources
12. Opens up leadership opportunities
13. Provides appropriate rewards and recognition

Guidelines for Gender Equity in Sports

Gender equity in athletics requires more than an equal number of offerings. It also requires equivalent efforts and considerations in the following areas:

- Level of competition
- Length of season (number of contests)
- Access to practice facilities
- Locker room accommodations
- Number and quality of coaches
- Budget allocations
- Supplies
- Uniforms
- Travel accommodations
- Quality of officiating

Fiscal fitness requires that the activity program become as fully self-supporting as possible. This means managing costs, setting reasonable and realistic participant fees and ticket prices, and limiting the number of activities offered.

Adding and dropping sports or other activities as necessary to balance student needs against existing budget parameters is the key to a sane and solvent program. Parents, students, and coaches can't do this. School boards won't do it. Administrators have to. That's why they pay you the big bucks. You should consider the following when expanding or eliminating sports or other activities:

- Level of interest
- Costs
- Availability of qualified coaches
- Impact on gender equity
- Opportunities for competition
- Level of community support
- Prospects for long-range continuation
- Transferability of skills to lifelong activities

- Other schools' experience with the activity
- Conflict or lack of conflict with other activities

Once you've arrived at the optimum number of sports, clubs, and other activities to fit your school's needs, you can stretch your activity budget even further through economies of scale (e.g., buying athletic equipment and supplies in bulk during the offseason) and by scaling back personnel costs through the use of volunteer nonfaculty coaches and advisors when appropriate. At Champlin Park High School (Minnesota), even the governor of the state has volunteered as a coach. If it works at Champlin Park, it can work in your school as well.

Every student activity program, including yours, can be run with greater cost-saving efficiency. It doesn't take superior knowledge or expertise. It's mostly a matter of will. Some administrators have it. Some don't. What about you?

How to Run an Effective Staff Development Program on a Shoestring

Staff development isn't a frill. It's a necessity. All teachers have to engage in continuous professional growth. Kids deserve it. The public expects it. It's the principal's job to see that it happens. But does it have to cost an arm and a leg? More and more school leaders don't think so.

Some schools don't spend any money on staff development. They're wrong. Others spend huge sums on in-service training. They can be wrong, too. It isn't how *much* money is spent on improving staff effectiveness; it's *how* the money is spent.

Some schools put most of their staff development resources into securing nationally known inspirational speakers and staging glitzy, multimedia presentations. Such programs can be moving, informative, uplifting, and entertaining; but they usually have minimal lasting impact on the classroom.

One-shot programs, no matter how sophisticated, seldom have life-altering effects on teachers. There are better ways to get the biggest bang for your buck.

The whole purpose of staff development programs is to help teachers make better decisions in the classroom. These programs need to deal with nitty-gritty issues that teachers care about and provide insights and information that teachers can put to use in their classrooms. The information must also be delivered by sources that the teachers accept as credible.

With this in mind, many school leaders are finding that they can run an effective staff development program literally on a shoestring as long as they follow these basic guidelines:

1. The program should be personalized and tied to building goals.

2. All staff members involved should participate in identifying growth needs and developing relevant programs. Ownership is a precursor to commitment.

3. Individual and group needs should both be addressed.

4. Learning experiences should deal with both the *science* and the *art* of teaching. Programs should include opportunities for both *professional* (theory, knowledge, skills) and *personal* (health, wellness, morale, enthusiasm) growth.

5. Programs should give teachers reasons for doing things differently.

6. Teachers need to see some payoff for participating in staff development programs. The WIIFM factor (What's In It For Me) is important to program success.

7. Effective programs include choices.

8. Programs should reflect an understanding that not all teachers learn alike. Teachers have varied learning styles just as students do. The best staff development programs include a variety of delivery systems and formats.

9. Programs must allow for continuous feedback, follow-up, and follow-through.

10. Teachers learn best from other teachers!

If you agree with most teachers that these are the characteristics of an effective staff development program, you can forget about bringing in Dr. Big Name National Expert for a daylong, all-staff tent meeting. Save your money. Your staff development dollars will be better spent on developing home-grown, homeowned strategies and programs for professional growth.

The best staff development programs occur at the building level. If funds are limited, put your money in grassroots efforts that are most likely to have both immediate and long-range effects that really make things better for kids. You can't spend money more wisely than that.

Following are seven simple "thrift-pack" suggestions for delivering high-impact, low-cost staff development opportunities for your teachers regardless of the school's size or budget:

1. Make the most of built-in, easily accessible resources such as local colleges, state departments of education, professional organizations, district specialists, and publishers' representatives. All of these sources are eager, willing, and able to help teachers improve at little or no cost to the school. It's too good a deal to miss out on.

2. Don't overlook the expertise on your own staff. Use in-house experts whenever possible. Your best teachers have a lot of experience, insights, knowledge, materials, and skills that can benefit other staff members. Sharing is what professionals do. Let it happen. That's homegrown staff development at its best.

3. If outside help is what you really need, share the costs with other schools that have similar needs. Never bring in outside consultants and foot the entire bill yourself.

4. Establish TATs (teacher assistance teams) within the school. Based on a collegial consultation model (see the box on p. 74), TATs create a support system for classroom teachers to facilitate building-level problem solving. Some of the best professional growth occurs when teachers learn from each other how to solve real-world issues. The basic premise behind TAT is simply that teachers can solve more problems working together than alone and can learn from each other in the process. The TAT model stresses maximum flexibility with a minimum of cost, time, or bureaucracy (see Form 3.1).

5. Capitalize on individual teacher attendance at professional seminars, conferences, and conventions. Too often when a teacher attends a professional meeting, the experience benefits only that individual. You can multiply the impact simply by requiring that all those who attend conferences bring back at least one "crazy" idea that can be shared with the staff and

implemented throughout the building. It doesn't cost any more to extend one person's experience to provide a growth opportunity for all.

6. Require all staff members to complete an Individual Professional Growth Plan for the year (see Form 3.2). The plan works for teachers just as the familiar, mandated IEP (Individual Education Plan) works for special education students. It's an action guide for intentional improvement. This kind of personalized staff development plan promotes individual growth and accountability. Best of all, it is easy, economical, and effective. Fiscal fitness doesn't get any better than that.

7. Tap into online mentoring programs for teachers. New e-mail mentoring systems, such as Mighty Mentors, created by Mighty Media, Inc., offers teachers global access to experts in their field. It's free. And it's available night or day. Cyberstaff development may be the wave of the future.

These are just a few of the many ways to foster staff development and conserve resources at the same time. There is one caution, however, about belt-tightening in this area.

The TAT Model

- One or more teacher teams are selected by the staff. Membership may be rotated among interested and willing veteran staff members.
- Classroom teachers refer specific individual problems to the team for advice and assistance.
- After reviewing the problem, the team meets with the referring teacher to define desired outcomes, generate alternative solutions, and establish timetables and evaluation procedures.
- The referring teacher selects the most viable solutions and tests them in the classroom.
- Follow-up meetings with the team are held as necessary to assess progress or brainstorm additional options.

Form 3.1 Sample TAT Assistance Request Form

TAT Assistance Request Form

Teacher's Name: _____ Grade or Course: _____

1. Describe the curriculum, instructional, or behavior problem
   (be specific):

   _____

   _____

   _____

   _____

2. State desired outcome:

   _____

   _____

   _____

   _____

3. What has been tried so far?

   _____

   _____

   _____

   _____

4. Other background information:

   _____

   _____

   _____

   _____

Date: _____ Signature: _____

Form 3.2 Sample Individual Professional Growth Plan

Individual Professional Growth Plan

Name: _____ Assignment: _____

My choice(s) for my personal professional growth plan for the year are indicated below.

I. _____ I will enroll in the following college or inservice courses:

    a. _____

    b. _____

    c. _____

II. _____ My professional growth plan will include leadership/service on the following committees or task forces:

    a. _____

    b. _____

    c. _____

III. _____ I want to follow a customized professional growth plan this year as described below (include selected topic and planned activities):

_____

_____

_____

_____

_____

_____

_____

Date: _____ Signature: _____

When pressured to economize, it may be tempting to cut back too much or to cut out the staff development program altogether. Such cuts are easy to make, and no one is apt to complain very much right away. But it's always a mistake.

If you are not consistently investing a reasonable amount of resources in teacher growth, you're short-changing the teachers, the kids, and the future of your school as well. There's a big difference between cutting out fat and cutting your own throat.

How to Save Money on Public Relations and Still Get the Job Done

If you are like many principals and superintendents, you may feel a little uncomfortable about school public relations programs. Marketing seems unprofessional to many educators. That's why some school leaders are always willing to cut back or cut out public relations first whenever times are tough. They couldn't be more wrong.

Public relations is just another name for purposeful, managed communication. This is something schools need more than ever. When myriad forces in society are continually bashing schools in public, the schools need the capability to set the record straight. When conditions are the worst, schools need public relations the most in order to tell their story, maintain morale, and rally support.

Never make any budget decisions that sabotage your ability to get your message across. Trying to balance the budget by sacrificing public relations functions is a classic example of being "penny wise and pound foolish." Cutting out resources for public relations isn't prudent fiscal management. It's suicide.

If you don't tell your school's story, who will? Every school needs an adequate public relations program. That doesn't mean that every school needs an expensive public relations program. There's no reason to fund a Madison Avenue campaign when a little mainstream marketing will do. Overkill is always an extravagance.

The best public relations programs succeed because of energy, effort, and openness, not expenditures. Here is a practical collection of surefire tips for conducting an effective, cost-conscious public relations program that can work in any school setting:

- Make the most of every media contact (see the guidelines on p. 80).
- Issue press releases and hold press conferences when needed. Politicians do it all the time. Why shouldn't school leaders? They are a free and effective way to communicate with the public.
- Get on local radio and television talk shows whenever possible.
- Capitalize on free use of public access cable television.
- Persuade your local newspaper to donate a column or page each week for school news.
- Solicit local businesses to underwrite the costs of printing and distributing a communitywide newsletter on school affairs.
- Maintain an up-to-date Web site. Student input can help keep it fresh and interesting.
- Start a speaker's bureau. Be ready and available to tell your school's story to any group, any time, anywhere. Urge your key staff members to do the same.
- Combine mailings with the city or other governmental agencies.
- Maintain a school hot line 24 hours a day.
- Showcase the school out in the community. Hold classes in a local mall where shoppers can observe. Conduct outdoor concerts in the neighborhoods.
- Dare to write letters to the editor. It's another free way to make your voice count.
- Become a fanatic about accessibility. Hold weekend and after-hours office hours.
- Display school newspapers and yearbooks in local physicians' and dental offices.
- Arrange to have school messages featured on billboards and marquees throughout the community.
- Make the most of parent-teacher conferences. Provide transportation on school buses, serve food, include grandparents, provide interpreters as needed, provide valet parking (high school students love this duty), ensure parking lot security, brighten up the school with banners and balloons, show vid-

eos of school activities. Do whatever it takes to get people out and to hold their attention once they are there.

- Convert an old school bus into a "Schoolmobile" to carry school exhibits and displays throughout the community.

- Schedule coffee klatches and brown bag seminars as a means of meeting with parents and the public.

- Conduct whistle-stop tours at the beginning of the school year. Have key staff leaders ride the bus, getting off at regular stops to visit with residents and answer questions.

- Hold neighborhood meetings in churches, parks, and fast food restaurants throughout the community during the year.

- Encourage local churches to include school items in weekly bulletins and parish newsletters.

- Establish voice mailboxes for all personnel, including the school board.

- Make creative use of the telephone. Try calling parents who are normally uninvolved in the school just to offer encouragement and answer questions.

- Produce videos on school activities and make them available to the public for checkout.

Every school has to find ways to get its story across to the public. Yours is no exception. Fortunately, as shown, this *is* possible to do, even with limited resources. Just be sure you do it!

It May Be Time to Milk the Sacred Cows

Most dictionaries define a sacred cow as something "immune from criticism, often unreasonably so." Every school has them. You know the programs in your school that fit this category.

When it comes time to stretch resources, cut costs, or find more creative ways to do business, these sacred cows are seldom scrutinized. They are presumed to be untouchable, indispensable, permanent. What's wrong with this picture?

The trouble with sacred cows is that things change—relentlessly. Values evolve. Priorities shift. Realities are replaced. Yesterday's necessities become tomorrow's irrelevancies. In times of chronic, chaotic change, sacred cows don't make much sense anymore.

Dos and Don'ts for Dealing With the Media

1. Focus on informing the public accurately, completely, and in a timely manner.
2. Be patient when answering questions from the media. Avoid using "no comment" as a response.
3. Don't try to second-guess the media as to what is and isn't newsworthy.
4. Despite media pressure, respect data privacy requirements.
5. Answer questions truthfully, without embellishments or editorializing.
6. Never lie to the media.
7. Don't bluff or guess. If you don't know, say so.
8. Tell the bad news first and quickly. Get it over with.
9. Don't stall. The media have deadlines.
10. Avoid jargon.
11. Always keep your promise to return calls to reporters.
12. Avoid off-the-cuff comments that may haunt or embarrass you later.
13. Talk to reporters in a natural conversational manner. Resist the urge to speak rapidly.
14. Don't ever assume that anything is "off the record."
15. Don't back away from microphones or cameras.
16. Don't allow reporters to lead you away from the subject.
17. Speak with authority, certitude, and conviction. Your goal is to establish the school as the most credible source of information about school matters.

When conditions make conserving resources the only option and all other efforts lead to dead ends, it may be time to milk the sacred cows. Sometimes fiscal fitness requires that nothing is sacred any longer.

When you're out of other choices, be brave enough to ask tough questions about the unquestionable (see examples). "Dare to go where no one else has gone before." It's what top administrators do all the time.

Challenging Sacred Cows: Sample Questions

Is a course in Latin still an absolute?

Is hiring little old ladies from the neighborhood to serve school lunch still cost-effective?

Does the prized local history course still merit a full year?

Is operating our own fleet of school buses still competitive?

Is our traditional seven-period day the best we can do?

Fiscal fitness doesn't mean always having the right answers, but, rather, asking the right questions. When you are willing to challenge the sacred cows in the organization, you are truly ready to "do more with less." No one said it would be easy. Only possible.

Note

1. This term refers to a fence posthole, which is narrowly defined, but deep. The term, a fairly common one in the Midwest since the 1950s, indicates opportunities for students to occasionally take time to go into great depth on a specific topic.

4

How to Get Everyone
Involved in Fiscal Fitness

School budgets are never enough. That's why all schools need outside help if they are to make do with what they have and still meet society's expectations. Because public schools belong to everyone, everyone has some obligation to help. Of course, *help* can mean a lot more than just paying taxes every year.

There are a lot of other ways that individuals, groups, organizations, and entire communities can pitch in to ensure that their schools remain fiscally fit. It's up to principals, superintendents, and other school leaders to find ways to get everyone involved. Tapping community resources is the only way for schools today to do their job and make ends meet.

Getting other people to help you get more out of your school's budget is no mean trick. It doesn't occur by accident; and they don't teach it in graduate school. But all the keys to greater community participation are spelled out in this chapter.

The following ideas for building partnerships and collaboratives, increasing active citizen involvement, and getting communities to reclaim more responsibility can be implemented in any school—including yours. Try them. They work.

How to Build Business Partnerships
That Really Pay Off

Business leaders have always been vocal in criticizing the schools and their products. Fortunately, more and more businesses today are realizing that they have a vital stake in the schools that prepare their future customers and workers and that they have the opportunity and the obligation to become part of the solution. It's not enough anymore for business representatives to merely criticize from the sidelines. Consequently, more and more schools are now finding that they can literally do more with less by forming effective partnerships with the business community.

In the past, school-business partnerships were hit-and-miss, trial-and-error, give-and-take relationships where one party (usually business) did all the giving and the other party (usually the school) did all the taking. Technically, these arrangements were more charity than partnering. This isn't true today.

Now most successful and productive school-business ventures are two-way streets. They involve much more than one-sided donations or sponsorships. They are true partnerships. Both parties are equal. Both derive specific benefits. That's the way the schools want it and that's what works best. When done properly, such a partnership becomes greater than the sum of its parts. There's no better way to stretch school resources.

Business partnerships can be simple or complex, but they don't have to be fancy to be effective. They run the gamut from informal, information-sharing relationships to more legal arrangements requiring formal joint powers agreements. Linkage levels between schools and businesses include

1. *Networking:* The parties build informal contacts around shared information and communication.
2. *Coordination:* The parties mesh efforts to capitalize on what each does best. Functions are realigned to make the best use of resources.
3. *Cooperation:* Each party relinquishes some identity and autonomy in exchange for certain specific benefits, such as cost savings.
4. *Collaboration:* The parties conduct a joint effort to reach a common goal. Both parties contribute resources to the solution of a mutual problem. The collaborative often becomes more important than the identity of the separate parties.
5. *Community partnership:* All stakeholders in the community join together to address a mutual problem, with each playing a specific role in the solution. A plan involving the total com-

munity must be developed. It must call for the participation of the schools, the business community, governmental units, local service agencies, and other service clubs and organizations.

Partnerships with businesses can be forged at the building or district level. Linkages that begin at the lowest level often evolve over time into full-blown partnerships. Naturally, none of these joint efforts is without its problems.

School-business partnerships are never trouble free. If they were, everybody would sign up. The three biggest impediments to carrying out successful joint efforts are the following:

- *Getting started*: "All beginnings are hard," according to author Chaim Potok. This may be especially true of partnerships. It's easy to talk about teaming up. It's a lot harder to overcome organizational inertia and actually take the beginning step. Who goes first? When? How?

- *Time*: Developing partnerships takes time. They won't succeed unless the principal or other administrator-in-charge takes the time to attend to all of the partners involved, to keep them fully informed, and to relentlessly seek their input.

- *Turf battles*: Identity, autonomy, independence, and self-determination are important to all organizations in both the public and private sectors. No school or business relinquishes them easily. Every instinct is to protect your turf against intrusion or usurpation. Yet breaking down boundaries is what partnerships are all about.

Fortunately, these and other common obstructions are just problems, not insurmountable obstacles. They can be overcome. It just takes willingness, commitment, planning, and some old-fashioned stubborn persistence.

It can't be too hard or there wouldn't be so many existing examples of successful partnering between elementary and secondary schools and businesses of all kinds and sizes. Some of the best and most common types of effective partnerships today include the following:

- *Adopt-a-school programs.* Probably the most widely recognized form of business partnership is the "adoption" of an individual school by a nearby business. Often the business will provide volunteers, field trip experiences, prizes and incentives for achievement, and extra equipment and supplies in exchange for the after-hours use of school facilities and technology.

- *Nursing home and elementary school partnerships.* Partnerships between nursing homes and primary schools are also common across the country. Typically, students visit the nursing facility on a regular basis, become "buddies" with the elderly residents, and celebrate birthdays and holidays with them. In return, the residents may share oral histories with the children and provide a venue for pupil performances.

- *Hospital and school partnerships.* Many schools work out arrangements with a local hospital whereby students perform such services as visiting and performing for patients, creating decorative art work for drab institutional walls or making entertaining videos for pediatric wards. The hospital, then, may sponsor school events, provide career resource speakers, and assist with school science fairs.

- *Shadow programs.* In many communities, the school and business community work together to provide opportunities for teachers to "shadow" businesspeople (walk in their shoes) and for business leaders to shadow teachers.

- *Ethics workshops.* Growing in popularity, some chambers of commerce join with schools in sponsoring an annual Ethics in the Workplace workshop for students and business leaders. The workshops are heralded as an effective bridge for connecting the generations and a lively learning experience for all parties.

- *Mentoring programs ("Two Together" programs).* Most cities now have mentoring programs in which local business people volunteer to guide and befriend children who are teacher or parent referred. Usually such programs involve at least twice-monthly contact and a year-long school connection. Mentors oftenreport getting as much or more out of the relationship as their young protégés.

- *Adolescent girls support groups.* As public awareness of the image issues confronting today's adolescent girls increases, special support groups are springing up around the country. In most such programs, women business leaders meet regularly with teenage and preteen middle school girls to interact with them about self-esteem concerns, career options, and survival skills for the new millennium. Besides the feel-good rewards of helping others, the payoff for the business participants is the chance to build positive relationships with potential future employees.

- *Career mentoring programs.* These programs typically match students interested in a specific career with appropriate business leaders for a six-week period of mentoring, shadowing, and working on special projects that benefit both the student and the business involved.

- *Community readers.* Reading stories to kids has always been fun for grown-ups. In many communities, the fun is just beginning. More and more business groups and service clubs are voluntarily coming into classrooms on a weekly basis to read aloud to primary school-aged children. In most cases, it's difficult to tell whether it's the students or the business representatives who enjoy it the most.

- *District-level partnerships.* Although many successful partnerships are developed at the building level, some of the most productive and far-reaching are linkages between the entire school district and a major local business or industry. Some of the best examples involve a major employer from the health community teaming up with the district on projects such as increasing immunization rates, providing asthma education, or setting up a free clinic for teenagers.

- *Fishbowl dialogues.* A recent development in school-business partnerships involves the participation of students in "fishbowl dialogues" (in which they interact with each other while being observed, as if in a fishbowl) about career interests, future plans, and school experiences, while being observed by local businesspeople. Afterward, interaction between the two groups often results in the identification of new business-education goals and partnerships.

These examples illustrate the endless variety of possible and potential business partnerships. Some partnerships are ad hoc. Some are ongoing. All make a difference.

Partnerships are a way around a fixed budget. They multiply your resources and make your school more capable than it was before. Forming partnerships with community businesses can change your school forever. It's a good change.

Although every partnership is different, most go through common phases of development. Whether you're interested in building a simple partnership at the building level or a more comprehensive one districtwide, the same 10 steps apply. Following are the 10 steps to effective business partnerships:

1. Identify a real-world, mutual problem, issue, concern, or goal to address.
2. Don't rush. Provide ample time for dialogue among all potential partners.
3. Agree on a specific, limited, and well-defined purpose.
4. Obtain commitment from the leaders of all participating groups.
5. Select a planning task force or group.
6. Develop an action plan, including definite assignments (division of labor—who does what) and a specific timetable.
7. Implement the action plan. All partners provide each other with necessary technical assistance and share relevant resources.
8. Promote the partnership. Share information with the community, build broad-based commitments, develop support, and gather additional resources.
9. Evaluate, adapt, and refine focus.
10. Routinize the partnership. Make it the normal way you do business from now on.

Obviously, the most successful partnerships spring from a concern the school and the business community share, such as drugs, gangs, the quality of vocational education, and the transition from the classroom to the world of work. Partnerships that are contrived or forced quickly fall apart.

There is no one right way to form a business partnership, and no partnership is perfect. Partnerships don't have to be. Any legitimate linkage—even if flawed—is a step toward better use of school and community resources. That's good for kids, good for the community, and particularly good for your school budget.

Use Collaboration As a Key to Cost Containment

Of course, not all partnerships have to be made with businesses. Schools can just as easily team up with other schools, governmental units, or nonprofit agencies to pool resources, cut costs, and achieve more than their individual budgets will allow. Some educators refer to these special partnerships as "collaboratives" to distinguish them from alliances with business partners.

Necessity can be the mother of collaboration. As Bridget Gothberg, past president of the National Community Education Association (NCEA), explains tongue-in-cheek, "Collaboration is an unnatural act between unconsenting adults." Sometimes, reluctantly and only when there is absolutely no other recourse, school personnel join forces with other agencies.

More often, however, collaboration is the result of creative leaders seeking innovative ways to do more with less. Through collaboration, public bodies can often accomplish more than they could ever possibly afford to do on their own.

Collaboratives commonly move beyond simple partnerships or ordinary interagency cooperation. In a true collaborative, everyone gives, everyone risks, and everyone "owns." Kids and taxpayers are the winners.

To illustrate, in the district where Gothberg serves as director of Community Education, the schools have entered into the following collaborative ventures and programs:

- *Meadowbrook Collaborative:* In this collaborative, the schools have joined with four other governmental and health community partners to upgrade the quality of life in a low-income housing complex. An outreach worker is housed in the neighborhood to work with residents to help them meet their health, educational, and safety needs. A "Cop Shop," a decentralized community policing station, is also located in the complex.

- *Adult Options in Education:* This collaborative unites three school districts in meeting the basic educational needs (English as a second language, GED, family literacy, and math tutoring) to help make them productive members of the community.

- *Project SOAR:* This interdistrict collaborative integrates adults with disabilities into existing learning opportunities and develops new opportunities where none currently exist.

- *Summer Meals:* Because hunger doesn't take a summer break, several community service agencies have banded with the school district to provide noon meals to needy students throughout the summer months. Instead of being served in the school cafeteria, the lunches are transported to parks, playgrounds, and neighborhood meeting rooms across the city.

- *Interdistrict Downtown School:* Sometimes schools join together to create an even better school. In this collaborative, nine districts have pooled resources to develop an interdistrict downtown school located in the heart of a metropolitan area. The school features intercultural learning and real-life learning labs in the arts, business, and government. The school is open to all students from the districts participating in the collaborative.

As the preceding examples demonstrate, effective schools never shy away from opportunities to work with like agencies to do more for more kids at less cost. Forming a collaborative with another public sector organization works the same way as developing a business partnership. Only the politics may be a little different.

Don't be too proud to collaborate. It's easier than you think. It's fun. It's the right thing to do, and your school board will love it.

Reach Out to Parent and Community Advisors

It's always important to reach out to businesses and other organizations for assistance in doing a better job without spending more money; but the best help is often closest to home. Parents are usually your most willing, able, and ready allies in achieving fiscal fitness. They have as great a stake in the school's success as you do; and they can do a lot more than just bake cookies or perform volunteer chores in the classroom.

Increasingly, school administrators are turning to parent and citizen groups for advice and counsel on matters affecting productivity and the efficient use of human and nonhuman resources in the school.

As the leader of the school, part of your responsibility is to make optimum use of all resources. And parents are resources. When you have CEOs, money managers, budget makers, human resource specialists, trend-spotters, and other experts in your parent pool, how dumb is it not to use them?

Schools have always relied on parents and citizens for advice and recommendations. Today, however, the best principals and superintendents have taken advice-seeking to a higher level. In some schools, it's become an art form. Many administrators now have a whole array of advisory groups to help them solve specific problems, stretch revenues, become more entrepreneurial, seek out new resources, and make wiser budget choices.

Some of the most common types of school advisory groups include the following:

- PTA/PTO executive boards
- Curriculum advisory committees
- Parent advisory councils
- Parent communication networks
- Vocational education advisory committees
- Athletic advisory councils
- Community education advisory committees
- Finance advisory committees

These groups not only can help the school make good spending decisions, they add credibility and clout to efforts to gain support for economies and other fiscal fitness measures.

Making effective use of parent and citizen advisory bodies has become a survival skill for school administrators. It is always worthwhile, although not always easy.

Common Stumbling Blocks
for School Advisory Councils

1. An ill-defined purpose
2. A membership that is too large or too small
3. A nonrepresentative membership
4. Bad timing (being established prematurely or too near the end of the school year)
5. Lack of resources (e.g., funding, clerical support) for the council
6. Information overkill (too much information too soon)
7. Internal politics
8. Inadequate provision for evaluation
9. Council recommendations that leave the staff no choices or alternatives
10. Lack of follow-up

To make the most of parent-citizen committees, task forces, and advisory councils, veteran administrators suggest the following steps:

1. Define the areas of responsibility. Be sure that everyone involved understands what the term *advisory* means.
2. Limit the focus. Define specifically what the committee or task force is charged with doing. There are many possible functions:
3. Determine if the group is to be ad hoc or ongoing.
4. Prescribe membership requirements and parameters (representation, term limits, selection procedures, etc.).
5. Identify leadership.
6. Establish operating rules or bylaws if necessary.
7. Provide adequate and appropriate resources, including materials, budget, and background information.
8. Arrange for necessary record keeping and reporting.
9. Set time limits and target dates.

10. Provide direction, help, and cheerleading as necessary.

11. Develop a process for keeping track of committee progress. Never allow an advisory group to drift or feel abandoned.

12. Evaluate every committee separately.

13. Get out of the way.

Parent Advisory Committee Functions

The most common functions of school advisory committees are

- Questioning/inquiring
- Examining/studying
- Conducting research/gathering data/fact finding
- Synthesizing
- Identifying problem areas
- Prioritizing
- Informing
- Suggesting/recommending
- Evaluating
- Reporting results or outcomes

When used professionally, advisory committees and councils can work well as sounding boards and sources of new ideas. But sometimes that's not enough. That's why more and more schools are now taking the next step toward involving parents and citizens in on-site decision making by establishing site management councils that are quasi-governing bodies.

School-based management takes the concept of parent participation a quantum leap beyond the traditional advisory council. Where site councils exist, parents function as much more than advisors. They become equal decision-making partners.

A full-blown site management system features decentralized, participatory decision making that is carried out by a site council comprised of administrators, teachers, students, parents, and other community members. The purpose is to give all members of the school community a greater voice in the operation of the school by delegating authority for budgeting, spending, staffing, programming, and more. The rationale is that shared decisions are better decisions.

If you are willing to trade off some autonomy for the benefits of collective wisdom, a site management council is a viable model for improving your school's productivity. It's essential to remember, however, that only the principal or superintendent can and will be held responsible and accountable for the group's choices and decisions.

No administrator—not even you—has a monopoly on knowledge. You can never be sure you have done enough to get the most out of available resources until you've tapped all the best thinking available to you. That's why advisory committees and site councils are growing in popularity.

You don't have to have all the best ideas for saving money and doing things better and cheaper all by yourself, but you do have to know where and how to look for them and to be able to recognize good ideas when you find them. Reaching out is part of your job. Don't hold back.

How to Get the Community to Shoulder More of the Responsibility

Schools often cost more than they should because they are expected to do more than they should. In America, as in no other country, society has gotten into the bad habit of sloughing off more and more social problems onto the school to handle or resolve. It's not working. Adding more responsibilities without adding more dollars is a surefire recipe for failure.

Most schools could easily live within their means if they could rid themselves of the excess baggage society has saddled them with. Sound radical? A growing number of respected school leaders don't think so. Many outspoken principals and superintendents are now advocating that the schools draw the line, define what they do best, do it, and challenge communities to reclaim responsibility for functions that have little or nothing to do with the mission of public education.

Every time the home or larger community takes back a nonessential function or activity, the school can reallocate resources to do its real job better. That's fiscal fitness!

Of course, there are some people who say it can't be done. They must be wrong; because it's already happening in some districts. Following are a few examples of responsibilities that some schools have shifted or are shifting back to the home or the community:

Function	Responsible Party
Baseball program	Little League, American Legion Baseball
Other minor sports	Recreation department or community traveling squads
Driver education	Commercial vendors
Psychological services	Health care providers
Special interest clubs	Scouts and other youth-serving agencies
Social dance instruction	National Cotillion Academy
Sex, drug, and tobacco education	Family, churches, and health community
Security	Police department
Vocational education	Business, labor, and apprenticeship programs

Wherever the community steps in to relieve the school of a responsibility that can and should be shouldered elsewhere, teachers and administrators have more time and money to do what schools are supposed to do. What would happen if you challenged your community to get more involved by taking over added functions? You might be pleasantly surprised.

As communities reassume responsibility, it is simply another extension of the well-worn African proverb: "It takes a whole village to raise a child." This just might be the last, best way to restore fiscal fitness to the nation's schools.

If all individuals and groups do their share, the schools should be able to focus more and to have more to devote to true teaching and learning. A growing number of communities across the country are trying to figure out how to do it. If it's not happening where you live, it should be. Here's how it works.

Under banners such as "Children First," "All Kids Are Our Kids," and "We Love Our Kids," literally hundreds of communities nationwide have launched initiatives to engage all individuals, families, institutions, and organizations in giving children and teenagers the care and support they need to survive and thrive in a free society.

But how can a whole village actually work together to raise its children? Thanks to the Minneapolis-based Search Institute, we now know how to do it.

Through its groundbreaking research of the 1990s, Search has identified 40 crucial internal and external developmental assets that all young people need in order to achieve their full potential and avoid such at-risk behaviors as tobacco, alcohol, and drug use. The more of these assets children and teenagers have, the more likely they are to succeed in school and in life.

The assets pinpointed by Search have consistently proved to be essential building-blocks for students' positive growth and development, as well as powerful shapers of their lifestyle choices. These assets are concrete experiences and qualities that fall into eight broad experiential categories: (a) support; (b) empowerment; (c) boundaries and expectations; (d) constructive use of time; (e) commitment to learning; (f) positive values; (g) social skills and competencies; and (h) positive identity and self-valuing. Examples of the 40 life-altering assets include

- Family support
- Caring neighborhoods
- Parents' involvement in school and in their child's life
- Adult role models
- Family, school, and community boundaries
- Constructive use of time at home
- Resistance skills
- Sense of purpose
- Optimism about the future

How, then, can a community band together to raise healthy, strong, competent, and resilient adults? Make everyone—not just parents and teachers—an asset builder. Sound difficult? It is. But it is beginning to happen in large cities, suburban communities, and rural areas all across the country.

Where asset-building initiatives are most successful, they share the following characteristics:

- Their goal is to instill the 40 assets in all children.
- They emphasize proactive individual and collective community action (rather than penalties, punishment, and rehabilitation after the fact).

- They empower and support people of all ages to be asset-builders.

- They strive to build community involvement one neighborhood at a time.

- They don't rely on a set of canned solutions or predetermined reforms. Instead, they invite all parties to figure out how they can best contribute.

- They are rooted in an attitude, rather than in a belief in any specific program.

- They encourage all adults to think like a parent and care like a parent.

- They stress the importance of all individuals, families, and institutions (including government and the religious community) to support each other in creating a child-friendly environment in which all kids can live, learn, grow, and contribute.

In a nutshell, the initiatives that work best are essentially a call to all adults to reclaim responsibility for young people and to do their part in providing the guidance, support, and attention all children need to flourish. The spirit of these communitywide efforts is summed up in this statement by an active asset builder:

> We have both a responsibility and a hope. The responsibility is shared obligation we own for the well-being of our children and youth. It is the day in, day out responsibility to see that the young people of the community have what they need to thrive that is parceled out among parents, extended families, schools, synagogues and churches, family service agencies, city and state government, and health systems.
>
> The hope leads us out beyond this shared responsibility toward the vision of a community of concern for kids that encompasses people from every walk of life and every neighborhood corner. The vision is for a future where all members of the community participate with intentional awareness in a network of mutual ties, values, and trust that supports all kids.
>
> —Pastor Dennis Ormseth, Chairman, Children First

As asset-building is accepted as everyone's job, not just that of the home and school, schools have fewer problems, more manageable responsibilities, and enough resources to go around.

The following real-life examples illustrate ways in which communities are taking part of the burden off the schools:

1. Volunteer citizens supervise children at bus stops to ensure their safety.
2. Business leaders devote time each week to serve as mentors, readers, and role models for elementary children.
3. Members of the community band collect used instruments for the school's music program.
4. Investment advisors set up a fund to help needy students.
5. The city provides police liaison officers to maintain security in schools.
6. Parents commit to reading to their children and/or listening to their children read 22 minutes a day ("Catch 22").
7. Local physicians assume responsibility for improving immunization rates.
8. Community medical professionals assist school nurses in providing students from low-income families with intermittent prescriptions, glasses, hearing aids, contact lens cases, and watches with alarms for reminding them to take medications.
9. City government involves students in community service by giving them responsibility for helping to design playgrounds and local hiking/biking trails.
10. Hospital and medical personnel set up a free clinic for students staffed by volunteers.
11. Neighbors volunteer to supervise warming houses to extend ice skating hours for students.
12. Firefighters who are not on call monitor school zones during dismissal hours.
13. Police and firefighters assist in serving school lunches. It builds relationships and relieves the school's food service staff.
14. Local business employees tutor students during the summer months to prepare them for returning to school.

15. Local restaurants train students in food preparation, service, and management.

16. Churches offer free or low-cost after-school care for children of working parents.

17. Local service stations allow students to use their facilities for car wash fundraising events for school groups.

18. Adult volunteers ride "shotgun" on school buses to promote positive behavior and safety.

19. Professional musicians volunteer as piano accompanists for school plays.

20. Businesses adopt family-friendly policies to permit employees to attend school functions.

21. Churches initiate after-school programs featuring experiences and opportunities in drama, improvisation, woodworking, and storytelling. (When outside organizations sponsor these activities, the schools don't have to.)

Marshalling community resources for kids cranks the concept of partnership up a notch. In some communities, businesses are encouraged to sign a "Partnership Promise" stipulating what they are committing to do to help build assets in children and youth (see Form 4.1).

All it takes for an asset-building initiative to be successful is permission, encouragement, opportunity, and support. Everybody can help out in some way. No effort is too small or insignificant. It can work in any community. It's already occurring in many.

When everyone helps make things better for kids, the school's job is easier and school resources go further. That's how getting all parties involved in fiscal fitness makes everyone a winner. There aren't many better deals than that.

How to Get Students to Help You Do More With Less

It's not just business partners, community organizations, parents, and other adults who can help the school get more for its money. Students can help, too. Whatever students do for themselves by themselves can reduce the drain on other resources of the school.

Form 4.1 Sample *Partnership Promise* Form

Partnership Promise

Organization: _____

Contact Person: _____

Address: _____

_____

_____ Zip: _____

Phone: _____

Our organization promises to do the following (be specific):

- _____
  _____
  _____

- _____
  _____
  _____

- _____
  _____
  _____

- _____
  _____
  _____

Date: _____   Signature: _____

Please submit to Chamber of Commerce Business Council

Following are 10 easy ways that students can contribute to fiscal fitness:

1. *Drug prevention.* In many schools, student athletes and other leaders have formed drug awareness teams to speak to younger pupils about the dangers of substance abuse. Little kids look up to and listen to older students. That's why student-operated drug prevention programs are often more effective than D.A.R.E. or any commercial curriculum or program the school might purchase.

2. *Achievement gangs and study groups.* Students can boost academic success and test scores, while reducing the need for remedial and makeup programs later on, by forming "achievement gangs" or study groups. When students support and help each other learn, everyone wins.

3. *Safety education.* In some communities, student members of local scout Police Explorer Posts have successfully assumed responsibility for teaching safety to younger children.

4. *Peer counselors and mentors (natural helpers).* When selected students are trained to use peer counseling, mediation, and conflict resolution techniques to resolve student disagreements, often confrontations and violence decrease significantly. When students help students settle disputes peacefully, discipline problems diminish, safety ensues, school morale improves, and young people learn important life survival skills.

5. *Peer tutors/mentors.* Tutors don't have to be adults. Some of the most effective tutors and mentors are older students who help their peers or who volunteer to be "buddies" with younger children. Best of all, everyone benefits. Student tutors often learn as much as or more than their protégés.

6. *Student readers.* One of the best low-cost ways to improve reading scores and spark interest in reading in elementary pupils is to have older students read to them on a regular (weekly) basis. Girls and boys athletic teams frequently take this on as a service project and as a way to give back to the school. It doesn't hurt that it provides positive P.R. for the team and promotes their sport as well.

7. *Minorities helping minorities.* Some schools have had dramatic results by recruiting minority student leaders to mentor, monitor at-

tendance, and befriend other minority students who are having trouble in school. Such efforts often prove to be the most cost-effective way to improve behavior, attendance, and grades all at the same time and take some of the load off the school staff as well.

8. *Graffiti cleanup.* With cleaning supplies provided by city and police officials, students in many areas have taken over responsibility for painting over graffiti in the school. Graffiti is contagious. If not removed promptly, it encourages more defacement of property. That's why student activists are often willing to work on volunteer cleanup crews. It's a matter of school pride for the students and a big savings for the school.

9. *Student office aides.* It's nothing new for students to voluntarily help out in the school office in exchange for credit or just for the experience. It can prove beneficial for the students and save the school the expense of hiring additional office help. The only caution is that the experience should result in worthwhile learning for the students, rather than just exploiting free labor.

10. *Student welcome wagon.* It's not uncommon for individual students or groups of students to take over the task of welcoming and orienting students who come new to the school throughout the year. The students enjoy showing newcomers the ropes and showing off their school at the same time. In return, it saves the school staff some precious time.

These are just a few of the ways that students can be resources for the school, not just consumers of the school's resources. There are many more ways.

When you are trying to get everyone into the act of stretching your school's budget, don't overlook the students. Their energy and ingenuity can be invaluable in helping you to spend less without settling for less.

Other Organizations That Can Help

Fiscal fitness is a team sport. You and your school staff can't do all you want to do and need to do with the resources you have, unless you get help.

Fortunately, ample help is available in every community. Look for it. Ask for it. Break down doors to get it. Do whatever it takes to get all the help your school needs. It's what effective school leaders do.

In addition to business partners, interagency collaboratives, parents, ordinary citizens, and students, there are virtually dozens of existing groups and organizations in your area that can do part of your job for you or help you do your job better and cheaper. You haven't fulfilled your part of the bargain until you've tapped them all.

Following is a representative list of organizations that can help your school save more and do more:

Ministerial associations

United Way agencies

Service clubs (Rotary, Lions, Kiwanis, etc.)

Youth service agencies (YMCA, Boys & Girls Clubs, etc.)

Chambers of Commerce

Big Brother/Big Sister organizations

Family counseling and mental health clinics

Twelve-step programs (Alcoholics Anonymous, Alateen, etc.)

Child protection agencies

State departments of education

City, county, and state health departments

Vocational rehabilitation services

Police

Highway patrol

Sheriff

Colleges and universities

Mothers Against Drunk Driving (MADD)

State attorney general's offices

State teachers associations

MOMS clubs (organization of stay-at-home mothers)

Parent groups for challenged students (those with ADD, ADHD, EBD, LD, etc.)

Parents Anonymous

Teen parents support groups

Single-parent organizations

Pediatricians

Private and corporate foundations (funding sources—see Chapter 5)

Ad hoc task forces (such as a Governor's Task Force on School Violence)

Safe houses

Crime-Stoppers

Treatment centers

Bar Association

FBI

Employee unions

Alumni groups

Center to Prevent Handgun Violence

American Association of School Administrators (AASA)

National Association of Secondary School Principals (NASSP)

National Association of Elementary School Principals (NAESP)

Association of Supervision and Curriculum Development (ASCD)

State and federal representatives and senators

Retired teachers organizations

Faculty spouse organizations

Fellowship of Christian athletes

Homeless shelters

Future Teachers of America

4-H clubs

Civil Air Patrol

Junior Achievement

Amateur Athletic Union

American Field Services (AFS)

American Civil Liberties Union

American Council of the Blind

Association of Retarded Citizens (ARC)

Deafness Education and Advancement Foundation

Learning Disability Association

Legal Aid Society

American Association of Deaf Citizens, Inc.

National Center for Youth With Disabilities

PACER (organization of parents of special-needs students)

United Way

Public libraries

Phi Delta Kappa

National School Safety Center

Educational Research Service (ERS)

Neighborhood block clubs

National Institute on Drug Use

Jacob Wetterling Foundation (missing children organization)

National Institute on Alcohol Abuse and Alcoholism

Children's Defense Fund

U.S. Department of Education

National School Boards Association

Centers for Disease Control

This list is illustrative, not exhaustive. Every principal and superintendent should have his or her own list of local agencies and organizations that can help the school do more and be more.

The point is that asking for help is a sign of strength, not weakness. Get all the help you can. It's a leader's way.

Once you've tapped absolutely all of the resources available inside and outside of the school and if it's still not enough, the next step is simply to acquire more resources. You can get what you need. The next chapter explains how.

5

How to Find, Raise, and Attract Money in Hard Times

Fiscal fitness for schools isn't just about cost containment and getting a bigger bang for the buck. It's also about finding extra funding sources when you need them.

No matter how generous your school board is or how much of a budget-balancing genius you are, there will be times when available resources are simply insufficient. When the money runs out, your best recourse is to go out and get some more.

Fundraising and seeking out new sources of resources is a brand-new (and uncomfortable) role for many administrators. Get used to it. It's part of the deal in today's competitive educational marketplace.

Successful principals are increasingly accepting the fact that they have a heavy responsibility for fundraising and cultivating nontraditional sources of revenue. The best approach is to think of your school as an organization where the budget is *only one source* of financial support. There are many others, including partnerships, grants, gifts, fees, fines, and fundraisers. Effective leadership, then, becomes a matter of developing specific short-term and long-term goals and identifying designated funding sources that match up with each goal.

Even though public schools are not structured for profit making, they can become money magnets. There are plenty of "cash cows" out there if you know where to find them and how to milk them. If you don't know, you'd better learn. This chapter will help.

Today's successful school leaders don't have to be born with a Midas touch; but they do have to function as resource mobilizers. It's a skill that can be learned.

More than ever before, principals and superintendents need to be resource brokers and fund finders if they want their schools to succeed and excel. Colleges and universities have known this for a long time. How much time does the president of your alma mater spend courting new resources? Take a cue from higher education. It's your turn now.

The good news is that it's not as onerous a task as you might believe. Look around. The best schools you know about are a lot more entrepreneurial than most people realize. Many are creating mini-businesses that go far beyond old-fashioned fundraisers. There are success stories in schools all around the country. You can do this, too.

The first lesson to learn is that the key to generating extra income for your school is visibility.

The Visible School Gets the Gold

Some schools always seem to get a lot more than their share of the pie. They consistently receive a disproportionate amount of publicity, special attention, donations, contributions, seed money, grants, and discretionary funds. How do they do it? Visibility!

Your school will never move to the head of the line for extra funding unless people know about it. The school with the greatest positive visibility throughout the community and beyond usually gets the gold.

Effective administrators make sure that their school or district gets noticed. It pays to have the movers and shakers, who have access to extra resources, become familiar with you and your school. When important and influential people think and talk about good schools, you want to be certain that it's your school they think of first.

Naturally, most people won't know about your school or how good it is unless someone tells them. As school leader, that's your responsibility. Never be afraid to market your school. There are no trophies for humility. Community members with deep pockets can't support what they don't know about.

Seize every opportunity to promote your product. Make friends with the media. Be prolific in providing news tips and issuing press releases. Be accessible. Answer questions. Be honest. Always return reporters' calls. Credibility with the media is currency you can cash in when you need it.

Rapport with local, state, and federal legislators is also a valuable commodity. Be your own best lobbyist. Don't be a stranger to law makers. They can be invaluable allies when you go after government or foundation grants or need special favors.

It's even more important to get noticed by the powers-that-be close to home. People in authority (i.e., superintendents and school boards) tend to reward and support those leaders and those schools that attract attention to themselves.

Leaders whose schools receive positive attention and the advantages that go with it know how to make their schools stand out. It doesn't happen by accident. Of course, there are both right and wrong ways to go about getting noticed.

Obviously, scandals attract attention, but don't produce any positive benefits. Likewise, some administrators make the mistake of trying to use politics to gain favor or preferential treatment from the front office or the boardroom. Some writers call it the process of "assmosis"—the act of sucking up to superiors. It doesn't work and usually backfires.

Better ways to get noticed by those who control the district's purse strings are to be the first to try something new and exciting or to be the best at something the community values. Build on strengths. Celebrate successes. Focus on good news. It's good business.

Attention attracts more attention. Awards, grants, bequests, and gifts attract more of the same. When it comes to securing extra funding, visibility pays off. Make the most of it.

Go Where the Money Is, Tell Your Story, and Have a Wish List

Heightening your visibility as a school leader isn't showing off. It's an effective and legitimate means of trolling for extra dollars for your school. Extending your school's reputation throughout the community can help generate the financial help needed to support unfunded and underfunded programs and services.

To use visibility to the greatest advantage in attracting new sources of revenue, start by going where the money is. Join the Chamber of Commerce and local service clubs. (The weekly meetings of the Rotary, Lions, and Kiwanis clubs are packed with potential benefactors.) Get to know your school's most successful and influential alumni. Identify those merchants and others in the community who consistently support school causes. Find out who the local philanthropists are. Cover all the bases. You never know where you will strike gold.

Be shameless about telling your school's story. Let people know the good things that are happening for kids. Always be available to speak to civic groups of all kinds. Showcase student talent at community meetings and events whenever possible. Don't just talk about triumphs. Share the school's problems and frustrations (without whining) as well. How else can you get support for desired solutions?

Most important of all, always have a wish list handy. Opportunity comes to those who are ready to receive it. Be ready. If you don't know what to put on the list, your teachers can fill one out for you in a hurry.

When school leaders are visible enough long enough, sure enough they hit pay dirt. It can happen to you and your school.

Don't Forget About Fines, Fees, and Fundraisers

Although it's always important to keep your antennae tuned to the community for possible new sources of support, it's equally essential to tap the full potential of moneymaking opportunities within your own school. Creative administrators are frequently amazed by the amount of money they can generate through fines, fees, and fundraisers. Others think that these sources of income are distracting and too much trouble to bother with. Strangely enough, these are often the same school officials who never seem to have enough resources to do what they want to do.

Most schools impose fines on students for a variety of offenses ranging from overdue library books to lost locks to parking lot violations. Student fines usually serve multiple purposes. They get students' attention. They send a message. They serve as a reasonable penalty for minor infractions. And they generate a little extra money for the school.

No school ever got rich from student fines; but no school ever complained about having a little extra cash on hand from such fees either. Every little bit helps.

Charging fines isn't crass exploitation. It's just good business—and also a good learning experience.

Unlike fines, student fees can generate a fairly substantial amount of income for the school. Many schools today charge fees for sports and other extracurricular activities, user fees for participation in optional programs (e.g., driver's education), field trip fees, and supply fees for materials students use to create products they keep (e.g., art and woodworking projects). Some schools even charge a transportation fee for riding the school bus a short distance or for using the school's late-activity bus. In a growing number of schools, student fees actually make up a significant portion of the athletic department's budget.

Sample High School Athletic Participation Fee Schedule

Cheer team	$40
Cross-country running	$45
Football	$65
Soccer	$55
Swimming/diving	$45
Tennis	$45
Volleyball	$50
Basketball	$50
Gymnastics	$50
Hockey	$95
Nordic ski team	$50
Baseball	$55
Golf	$45
Softball	$55
Synchronized swimming	$50
Track and field	$45

Junior High School Athletic Participation Fee Schedule

All sports	$35

If there is any question or problem with fee payment, please contact the athletic director's office. Waivers and scholarships are available. No student will be denied participation due to inability to pay.

Charging fees for school activities can be controversial. Is it fair to charge fees in a free public school system? The answer is "yes" if the fees are reasonable and affordable for most students and are the only way to provide optional opportunities that the community wants and supports.

Before imposing any fee, however, the following two conditions must be met:

1. Never charge a fee for any event or activity in which students are required to participate.
2. Never charge a fee unless some scholarship provision is available to those students who cannot afford to pay. No student should ever be denied access to any program or activity in the public schools because of inability to pay a fee.

When these caveats are satisfied, student fees can be a legitimate way to supplement the school's regular budget and do more for kids.

Don't feel guilty about charging reasonable fees when appropriate. You should feel guilty only if you fail to explore every possible means—including fees—for providing maximum opportunities for your students.

Although fees can please and fines are fine, fundraisers are where the serious money comes from. Old-fashioned fundraising ploys, such as sending kids out to sell candy or gift wrap, are minor league compared to what many schools are doing to bring in extra money today.

Fundraising is now big business, as more and more principals across the country are becoming entrepreneurs for their schools. The only limitations on school fundraisers today are the creativity and imagination of the educators, parents, and students involved.

There's nothing that makes a school feel more fiscally fit than bulking up its budget through vigorous, big-league fundraising. If you want to significantly add to your school coffers, just look around at how other schools are making money. Many successful schools raise literally tens of thousands of dollars each year to use at their discretion. Your school can, too.

If you need help getting started, following are 25 examples of nontraditional fundraisers that have been successful in schools just like yours:

1. *Seed money.* Hold a garden seed sale. Gardening is the number one hobby in America today. That's too big a market to miss out on.

2. *Silent auctions.* When merchants and other patrons donate items for the school to sell at a silent auction, it's all profit.

3. *Chore corps.* When teenagers rent out their services to perform yard work, shovel snow, do housecleaning, and perform other chores for community members, everybody benefits. Grateful senior citizens and others can be extremely generous to the school.

4. *Magazine mania.* Some schools have had phenomenal success selling magazine subscriptions, instead of candy or cookies. It's not uncommon for a school to realize as much as $5,000 (or more) in profits every year. Best of all, getting repeat business is almost automatic.

5. *Black tie dinner and community ball.* In some communities, the highlight of the social season is the school's annual black tie dinner and fundraising ball. Many people are willing to pay to help the school and to have fun at the same time. Combine the event with a silent auction and you have a major moneymaker.

6. *Shopforschool.com.* Fundraising via the Internet may be the wave of the future. *Shopforschool.com,* a fledgling Web site in Minnesota, promises to give a percentage of its merchandise sales to the school of the shopper's choice. Fundraising can't get much easier. Once the program is operational, the school doesn't have to do any work at all. Part of the beauty of online fundraising is that grandparents and others can support the school of their choice from anywhere in the nation.

7. *Squeegee profits.* Some schools clean up several times a year by having athletic teams and other student groups stage a car wash at participating local service stations.

8. *Car bash.* You might be surprised at how many people will pay good money to work off frustration by sledge-hammering an old jalopy. Holding a "car bash" is a good way to raise money and promote mental health at the same time. It's worked everywhere it's been tried.

9. *Valet parking.* It's easy to multiply profits from the gate proceeds of popular school events simply by having students also provide valet parking for a small fee (tips also accepted). Parents like the

service. Kids like to drive the cars. And the school likes the extra money.

10. *Fashion statements.* Fashion shows are always a hit. Fashion shows featuring students wearing outfits and accessories on loan from local apparel merchants can also be big school budget boosters.

11. *Baby-sitters club.* All parents need a baby-sitter sometime. Have your school provide trained sitters with the fees going to support extra educational programs and activities.

12. *Halloween haunted house.* Although Halloween is banned in some schools because of its alleged historical connection to satanic celebrations, it is embraced in others as a fundraising opportunity. Operating a haunted house to entertain community children can be a great way to put the fun back into fundraising.

13. *Jail bail.* Take a tip from some well-established charities—use the "jail bail" approach to fundraising. It works by locking up prominent citizens, celebrities, and just plain folks in a mock jail and having them telephone friends and coworkers for donations to bail them out. It's a switch to have others do the asking.

14. *Bottled water.* Americans of all ages love their bottled water. That's why some schools have arranged with a local bottler to incorporate the school logo, name, and mascot on specially labeled bottles (e.g., Mustang Power Spring Water). These can be huge sellers to students, parents, sports fans, and other school supporters.

15. *School carny.* School carnivals aren't new, but some communities have added a few new twists to boost proceeds. For instance, a dunk-the-principal water tank is always a big draw and a big moneymaker.

16. *Kid's café.* Some schools are fortunate enough to have a local business owner willing to allow high school students to operate a restaurant for a night and keep the profits for the school. It's a good way to combine learning and earning. It just might work in your situation as well.

17. *Pi (Pie) Day.* If your math department needs some extra cash, sponsor a "Pi Day" during which students, staff, and community members compete in solving Pi*-related puzzles and problems

while purchasing and eating pies donated by local bakeries. Who says math can't be fun (and profitable)?

*Pi—π—is the number representing the ratio of a circle's circumference to its diameter—approximately 3.1459.

18. *Talent takeover.* A community talent show can mean money in the bank for the school. It worked for Mickey Rooney and Judy Garland in the classic movies of the 1930s and 1940s and is working in many places today. Production costs often run as low as 1% of what these shows bring in. That's a profit earnings ratio that any corporation would die for.

19. *Garage sale.* Garage sales are big business. Why not get your school in on the action? The Austin (Texas) schools have great success every year selling computers, VCRs, desks, globes, supplies, texts, and other items no longer needed by the school.

20. *A team approach.* A new idea in raising money for sports teams is being tried in a few communities across the country. Instead of asking people to buy products they don't want, student teams go door to door asking outright for tax-deductible donations. At the door, the athletes explain the program and ask for the donation of a certain dollar amount, say, $25. Each contributor receives a receipt for use at tax time.

In some cases, each sport does its own fundraising. In others, the fundraising efforts of all teams are consolidated into one campaign. Obviously, this experimental approach is controversial. Some people think it's too crass. Others think it's just straightforward.

21. *Student-alumni contests and concerts.* It doesn't take any market research to discover that athletic contests (e.g., in baseball, basketball, hockey games) between students and alumni are always popular with kids and adults alike. Often they are sellouts. Also growing in popularity are alumni concerts that reunite graduates with current band and orchestra students to perform together at holiday time or any time. Mixing fun and fundraising is always a winning combination.

22. *School videos and calendars.* Parents will buy almost anything with their child's picture in it. That's why many schools are successfully marketing school calendars featuring a picture of a different grade level each month; video tapes of games, concerts, homecom-

ing activities, commencement ceremonies, and other popular school events; and video yearbooks depicting school-year highlights. It's true that one picture is worth a thousand words. It's also true that sometimes one picture is worth a thousand dollars to the school.

23. *Coffee houses.* It's a quantum leap from knocking on doors selling candy to running a full-fledged business, but that's what has happened to many school fundraisers. Coffee houses are a good example. In a growing number of districts, students are learning invaluable lessons in entrepreneurship by actually operating a profit-making coffeehouse. A good case in point is the Galaxy CoffeeHouse in St. Paul (Minnesota), which is managed by Arlington High School students as a joint project of the school and a neighborhood council with all profits going into an educational fund.

24. *"Dough Raisers."* Arrangements with commercial vendors to sell pizza on school grounds during lunchtime are helping a growing number of schools to raise money, according to spokespersons for the Domino franchises. Some schools earn thousands of dollars from these "dough raisers." Companies, such as Dominos, actually adapt their recipes to meet federal school lunch requirements to help make these programs possible.

25. *Hometown MTV.* You know it's a new millennium when schoolchildren start recording and selling original albums to raise money for education. That's what's happened at Margaret Allen Elementary School in Nashville, Tennessee. (Where else?) Could this happen in your school community?

These examples make it clear that the options for school fundraisers are many and varied. There are some limits, however. Fundraisers can go too far, take too much time, distract too much, and even take unfair advantage of students. To avoid these extremes, many veteran administrators suggest adhering to certain fixed guidelines such as those on the next page.

Effective school leaders are never satisfied with the amount of money available to them. That's why school fundraisers are here to stay. If your school isn't raising its share of "extra" money, you're falling behind.

It isn't just God who helps those who help themselves. School boards, legislatures, and grant-givers do the same.

Fundraising Guidelines

1. Fundraising monies should be collected, dispersed, and accounted for by a third party (e.g., the PTA) whenever possible.
2. No fundraising activity should involve doing anything illegal (e.g., gambling in some communities).
3. No one should ever be embarrassed or intimidated by any school fundraising activity.
4. Every effort must be made to scrupulously avoid exploitation of the school's captive student population for purposes of fundraising.
5. Participation in all fundraisers must be completely voluntary.
6. Fundraisers should avoid false advertising or any conflict of interest.
7. All fundraisers must be completely nondiscriminatory.
8. Safety must be the top priority in all fundraising activities.
9. All fundraising events and activities should be in "good taste" according to community standards.
10. Involvement of students and staff in fundraising activities should be limited during regular school hours.
11. Money collected through fundraising must be spent for the stated educational purpose for which it was collected.
12. In all fundraising efforts, meticulous record keeping and accounting procedures must be followed. All records should be open to the public and subject to periodic independent auditing.
13. Where possible, monies collected through fundraisers should be kept in a separate bank account, and at least two signatures should be required to write checks on the account.
14. All fundraising projects should be educational and fun as well as profitable.

Make the Most of Educational Foundations, Alumni Associations, and Booster Clubs

In reference to charitable giving, John D. Rockefeller once advised, "Never think you must apologize for asking someone to give to a worthy objective." Rockefeller was right. As a school leader, you should never apologize for asking people to contribute beyond their tax dollars or hesitate to tell your closest supporters what you need and ask them to help you get it. If they won't help, who will?

For principals and superintendents, these "closest supporters" often include local educational foundations, alumni associations, and booster clubs. These are special partners that have a vested interest in the school's success and exist largely to promote the school and raise needed funds to augment the school's regular budget. They can be your best friends when it comes to fiscal fitness. It pays to make the most of them.

Booster clubs are frequently seasonal, activity-specific, and transitory. Different people are involved almost every year. They are most concerned with the here and now and the immediate future. They are most helpful when they have a specific, short-term goal, such as raising funds to send the marching band to this year's bowl game or to build a new weight room for the athletic department.

For best results, the most effective way to work with booster clubs is to appeal to their sense of pride in current school accomplishments and to treat them like who they are—most favored allies. Keep them informed about matters affecting their activity or program. Give the group credit for its contributions. Listen to their concerns and advice. Use them as a sounding board.

Most important, let booster clubs know how valuable and appreciated they are—but don't let them think they can run the activity or program they support. The school needs only one set of decision makers. That's you and your staff. Booster clubs should decide how to raise money for their cause. The professional staff should decide how to spend it.

Alumni associations are different in that they are interested not only in the present and future success of the school, but also in preserving the history, traditions, legacy, and memory of the school's "golden years" as they recall them. These associations are significant resources in major fundraising campaigns such as collecting money to upgrade technology throughout the school. They can be equally important as individuals who may be interested in bequesting money to the school for a variety of specific purposes—scholarships, for one.

Alumni like to be recognized individually for their past and present contributions. That's why there are so many laboratories, libraries, and other facilities named after them. Some schools even find it worthwhile to establish a Wall of Fame honoring generous graduates for their outstanding support. The tricks to getting the most out of alumni associations are: never take them for granted, never make frivolous requests, and never go to the well too often. Strangely enough, this is the secret to succeeding with any group of potential benefactors.

Of the three (foundations, alumni organizations, and booster clubs), foundations are the most legalistic and have the greatest potential for fundraising. Their goals are usually ambitious, long-lasting, and all-inclusive. Colleges and universities have always relied on foundations for fundraising. Public schools are just beginning to get into the act.

Most public school educational foundations are governed by formal articles of incorporation and well-defined bylaws. They are legally recognized nonprofit entities, organized and operated exclusively for charitable and educational purposes, governed by an elected or appointed board of directors and subject to strict accounting rules and regulations. Foundations may be formed jointly with the city or organized solely for the benefit of the school system or, sometimes, even for an individual school.

Typically, the mission of a public educational foundation is to:

- Engage in, advance, support, promote, and administer charitable and educational causes and projects of the school district (it's important to spell out that the foundation exists to support the school, not run it)
- Encourage and fund innovative ideas in teaching and learning
- Help ensure that the school provides a world-class education custom fit to the needs of the community and its children
- Build an educational endowment for the children of the community

Educational foundations can have the capacity to raise hundreds of thousands of dollars for schools. At the same time, they relieve school officials of a lot of the burden of fundraising. Don't even think about passing up a deal like that.

Where they exist, administrators are adamant that foundations are definitely worth the time and red tape involved. If you don't have an educational foundation in your community, look into starting one.

It could be the best thing that ever happened to your fiscal fitness program.

Get Busy and Go After
Grants, Gifts, and Endowments

If you're like many administrators who haven't had much experience with grantsmanship, you may feel out of your element in seeking or applying for grant money. If so, get over it. There is one compelling reason why you should get busy and go after grants and other awards—that's where the money is!

There are a lot of giveaway programs available to school leaders who know how to access them; but grant-givers won't seek you out. You have to go to them.

It's not just OK to use other people's money; it's the best way to stretch resources or do more with less. Every successful school leader today has to learn how to turn to outside funding sources, including private sector foundations and corporations, for extra financial support.

The good news is that grantsmanship isn't magic. It just takes a little know-how and a lot of hard work. It starts by understanding how foundations and other grant-givers function.

For newcomers to the competitive grant process, it helps to be aware of the differences between public grant sources (e.g., government agencies) and private sector foundations and corporate grant-givers.

Public grants are usually targeted for specific purposes and available only once a year. Private grants, however, tend to be more flexible and open-ended. Often, private foundations are more willing to consider experimental or off-the-wall proposals than government sources. Some private foundations are open to funding proposals two to four times a year, and a few actually have no specific deadlines, cycle, or schedule for application.

Most government agencies initiate the application process by issuing an RFP (Request for Proposal). Many corporate givers or private foundations, on the other hand, simply start by developing proposal guidelines, then waiting for submissions. In either case, applicants may be an individual school, a collaborative of two or more organizations, or an entire school district.

Although most educators are more familiar with government sources, private donors have been the hottest providers of grant money to schools in recent years. *Partnerships* is a popular buzzword in both education and corporate circles, and education is a top priority interest of many private sector foundations.

It's "cool" for the business community to give money to educational recipients today for a variety of reasons, including enhanced name recognition, tax advantages, and the opportunity to give back to the community or contribute to the solution of mutual problems.

All this is good news for educators; but school personnel must be wary of any attached strings. As some cynics warn, "When the partners dance, business likes to lead."

When pursuing private grant money, it pays to be aware that certain issues often receive priority consideration from corporate givers. These issues include the following:

School reform

Voluntary desegregation

Drug education

Technology

Drop-out prevention

Violence prevention

Business partnerships

Parental involvement

School choice

Gender issues

Antigang programs

Charter schools

At-risk students

Well-done proposals addressing these topics often stand a better-than-average chance of approval. (The key phrase is *well done*.) But there are no guarantees!

There's no mystery about the decision-making process of awarding grants. Certain elements are common to the majority of successful proposals. Following are what corporate grant-givers are looking for:

- Realistic goals tied to a reasonable budget
- Documentation of need
- Focus—clarity of objectives

- Originality, creativity, and uniqueness (something that sets the proposal apart)
- Linkage to the funder's needs, interests, or priorities
- Evidence of collaboration (some funding can only be accessed by working with other organizations, for example, with city government)
- Competent leadership with a successful track record in dealing with grant monies
- Replication potential
- Well-defined evaluation plans
- Provision for continuation of the project, program, or activity when outside funding ceases

Not all successful proposals contain all of these elements; but the more of them that are apparent in an application, the greater the likelihood of approval.

Developing grant proposals isn't an exercise in creative writing. Rather, it is following a prescribed format and filling in the blanks with facts. Most public and private funders request the same information in the same order. The anatomy of a typical proposal looks like the following:

1. Introduction (including applicant's location, enrollment, racial mix, solid-economic demographics, drop-out rate, grant experience, and mission statement)
2. Definition of need
3. Specific goals and objectives of the proposal
4. Proposed activities (project design)
5. Evaluation procedures
6. Budget (including salaries, fringe benefits, travel, supplies, materials, and contracted services)

Some grant-givers also require verification of tax-exempt status, IRS records, and information on the officers of the applying organization, including identification of a single contact person.

Budgets may be the meat and potatoes of the operation of the school; but grants are the gravy. The only bad thing about them is that not everyone gets them. Grantsmanship is a competitive process. There are winners and losers. The following insider tips can help you develop winning proposals and can give your application an edge over the competition:

- Begin by creating a culture that encourages aggressive grant-seeking.
- Take time to carefully research potential funders. Look for those whose priorities match your needs. Check regional foundation centers, which can be traced through your public library, and *The Foundation Directory,* which lists details of most major foundations.
- Use the Internet to find sources of grant money. Almost all federal agencies have information on the Internet, and most private foundations have a Web page.
- Subscribe to grants newsletters.
- Study winning proposals. Figure out what they did right.
- Don't think you can create a generic grant application that can be sent to all potential funders. Each source is unique. Tailor your application to the specific idiosyncrasies of each foundation or corporation (i.e., the HealthSystem Minnesota Foundation will only consider applications that help build specific "developmental assets" in youth). It can be useful, however, to develop "boilerplate" material (census data, test score information, etc.) that can be plugged into any application.
- Emphasize direct service in your application as much as possible.
- Try to establish a relationship with the people who control the purse strings. Learn how each funder prefers to be communicated with. Sometimes it helps to have your superintendent contact the CEO of the funding agency.
- Never ask for funds to supplant your regular budget. That's not what grants are for.
- Dare to admit problems. If you didn't have any, you wouldn't need extra grant money.
- Get letters of support from influential stakeholders.
- Get commitment in advance from those in the organization who will actually have to do the work if a grant is awarded. (Otherwise, you may be like a dog chasing a car —not knowing what to do with it if you catch it.)

- Include national statistics, research data, and the current thinking of experts in the field whenever possible.
- Follow all guidelines and instructions faithfully (number of pages, spacing, format, type size, etc.).
- Allow 1 to 3 months to assess needs and develop general ideas; 1 to 3 months to flesh out a proposal, search for a funding source, and make an initial contact; and 3 to 5 months to finalize and submit your proposal.
- Amend your proposal sparingly. Funders don't like surprises.
- Be patient. Waiting is the hardest part of the process.
- If rejected, get the readers' comments that give reasons for the disapproval.
- If approved, deliver what you promised and spend all the money. Funders don't like to get money back.
- Consider establishing a building-level Grantsmanship Team or a districtwide grants development office to help generate ideas, find appropriate funding sources, and train staff. Such offices often pay for themselves. Some experts estimate that in a 36,000-pupil district, a two-person (one administrator and one clerk) grants office has the potential of earning as much as $5 million in competitive grants over a 5-year period.

The strategies that work in securing grants can also help in attracting other endowments and awards.

Despite the complexity involved, don't be intimidated by the grant application process. It's not just large, well-known schools that get grants. Any school can. Yours can, too. But it won't happen unless you start making applications.

The best schools always have at least one grant in some stage of development or implementation. Can you afford to do less?

Should You Consider Selling Advertising?

Just how far schools can and should go to raise extra funds and attract outside money has yet to be determined. One of the most debatable emerging issues is whether or not schools should sell advertising.

Of course, schools have always sold ads in programs for sporting events, school newspapers, and yearbooks. But this has been largely viewed as penny ante and harmless. When huge sums of money are concerned, however, it doesn't seem quite so harmless anymore.

Some people believe that any time schools sell ads they are selling out their objectivity, integrity, and credibility. Others think it's just a logical marriage between free enterprise and free public education. In many communities, the debate is just heating up.

As costs escalate and the public financing that bankrolls most school operations falters or falls short, more educators are becoming willing to consider alternative moneymaking possibilities, including selling advertising.

The stakes are high. Sales of exclusive vending machine rights are now bringing in millions of dollars to school districts from Osseo, Minnesota, to Jefferson County, Colorado. It just so happens that there is big money in soft drinks if schools are willing to sell exclusive access to their captive student population. But it isn't just limited to soft drinks. In 1999, the Henrico County (Virginia) high school cafeterias took commercialism a step further by signing on as franchises for several fast food chains.

Other current forms of advertising in schools include renting display space for ads in gymnasiums and on school buses, endorsing products such as gym shoes, and revising lesson plans to use only certain products as examples.

There's no question that more and more schools are becoming advertising vehicles. Is it right? Wrong? Is it short-changing students' education to refuse to admit advertisements in school? How far is too far?

The final answers must lie with each community. What does your community think?

Why Not Run a School Store?

Most principals never planned to become shopkeepers; but that's what's happening in many places. A growing number of schools throughout the country are opening up school stores as a means of promoting school spirit, providing hands-on learning (a retail laboratory) for marketing students, meeting the convenience shopping needs of students, school personnel, and other patrons, and raising needed money for school projects and scholarships.

Often called Spirit Shops, these stores typically sell a variety of school-related items:

- School supplies (often decorated with the school emblem or logo)
- Spirit clothing and accessories (e.g., T-shirts, sweatshirts, caps, mittens, and ponchos)
- Stadium blankets
- Pennants and pom-poms
- Candy, soda, and baked goods
- Key chains, tote bags, and umbrellas
- Balloon bouquets
- Mugs, mascots, and other memorabilia

In some schools, the store is managed by distributive education students or marketing interns. In other situations, adult volunteers operate the school. Some school stores are open only before and after school and during lunch periods. Others are open daily during school hours, during special school events such as open houses or parent conferences, and for special holiday hours.

Because profit is only part of the purpose, most school stores have a relatively low mark-up (say, 30%) and give special prices for school-related projects and events. Nevertheless, profits can amount to $20,000 or more annually.

Operating a school store is one area where public schools should "go to school" at private and parochial schools that frequently run sophisticated merchandising programs. For instance, the Spirit Shop at Benilde-St. Margaret's High School in Minneapolis, run entirely by 25 parent volunteers and open from 11 a.m. to 3 p.m. every school day, realized a profit of $17,000 in 1998-1999.

If you're interested in opening a store in your school, it's wise to do some marketing research ahead of time, using a survey instrument such as the School Store Survey on the next page.

Your students and parents spend a lot of money on school supplies and paraphernalia each year. They might as well buy them from you.

Of all the ways that schools try to raise extra money, running a school store is not the most lucrative; but it may be the most educational and the most fun. If your school doesn't have a store, why not?

Form 5.1 Sample School Store Survey

School Store Survey

The Marketing Intern Class is considering opening a store in our school this year. This survey will help determine what items will be sold. Please check those items you would be interested in purchasing at school.

Beverages
__ Bottled soda
__ Bottled water
__ Hot chocolate
__ Bottled juice

Snacks
__ Granola bars
__ Sandwiches
__ Gum
__ Fresh fruit
__ Other (Specify_____)

School Supplies
__ Pencils
__ Folders
__ Paper
__ Erasers
__ Computer disks
__ Note cards
__ Other (Specify_____)

Personal Care Items
__ Deodorant
__ Shampoo
__ Lip moisturizer
__ Breath mints

School Spirit Stuff
__ T-shirts
__ Water bottles
__ Pom-poms
__ Polo shirts
__ Denim shirts
__ Golf towels

Clothes
__ Gym uniform
__ Sweatshirt
__ Other (Specify_____)

When will you most likely shop at the school store?
__ Before school
__ After school
__ Passing periods
__ During lunch

Help name the school store! The person who suggests the best school store name will win free movie passes and dinner at a local restaurant.

Name of store: _____

Your name and grade: _____

Please return this form to the principal's office.

Thank you!

Ramsey, R. *Fiscal Fitness for School Administrators.* ©2001. Corwin Press, Inc.

More Ways to Make Money for Your School

Running a school store is just one way to raise, find, or attract money for your school. This chapter has examined several others. Resourceful school staffs, like yours, can probably come up with many more.

If you run short of ideas, following are 10 more possibilities:

1. Copyright and sell locally developed curriculum materials.
2. Rent out computer labs and telephone banks for use by community groups.
3. Allow parents to raise private money to hire more teachers or specialists or to rehire staff lost to budget cuts. (Although it's common for parents to pay for special equipment or events, soliciting funds from them to hire personnel is a new, and controversial, approach. Opponents raise issues of inequity and parental interference. Advocates say, "Whatever works." Desperate times call for desperate measures. How desperate are you?)
4. Rent out vacant school office space.
5. Sell services such as printing or psychological testing.
6. Increase lunch prices.
7. Charge for your staff's consultation services to other districts and groups.
8. Become the Internet provider in your area.
9. Rent school buses and drivers to community groups for use during nonschool time.
10. Rent pool time or ice rink time to schools and groups that don't have these facilities.

The bottom line is that every school needs more money. Yours is no exception. It's impossible to build a better school simply by shifting priorities, downsizing, or stretching existing resources.

Every school has to create some of its own wealth. That's part of the fiscal fitness equation today.

Being an effective money manager will help you be a good school leader. Being an effective moneymaker will help you become an even better school leader.

6

How to Make the Most of Time — The Resource That Keeps on Ticking

What's the school's most precious resource? It's not money. It's time.

Time is the lifeblood of the organization. If you waste it, you can't get it back, and what you do with all your other resources won't matter much. On the other hand, if you make the most of the time you have, you are in the best position to make maximum use of all the other resources of the school as well.

The secret to time management is simply making good choices. How you choose to spend time is determined by how you think about it.

Change the Way You Think About Time

"Time is God's way of keeping everything from happening at once."

—Anonymous

Unless you understand the psychology of time, you can't make the best use of it. Too many educators (and other people) think of time the same way they think about the weather: It is something that everybody talks about, but no one does anything about. They're wrong.

Weather is fickle and often unpredictable. Time is constant. It's always there in the same amount, day in and day out. Weather is largely beyond our control. Time isn't. There are a lot of things people can do to manage their time.

127

Making time good to the last tick merely requires the right mindset. If you alter your frame of reference, you can start seeing time differently and start using it better.

Don't make the mistake of thinking of time as an enemy, an obstruction, or an arbitrary restraint. Time isn't negative. It's neutral. It is simply a working condition—another resource at your disposal.

Don't blame time (or the lack of it) for your shortcomings. If your school doesn't meet expectations, it's not time's fault. It's yours. It's easy to constantly whine that there isn't enough time. The truth is that there is time to do all that you absolutely have to get done.

Time plays no favorites. Superstars and also-rans have the same amount. Time doesn't make the difference between winners and losers. How they use it does.

Like other resources, time can be spent well or squandered; but it can't be multiplied, saved for later use, or invested. Time can't grow. It can only shrink. You can't borrow time or use someone else's. You're stuck with the time you have. It's the same for everyone.

That's why the best administrators don't obsess about time. They don't have to. They simply accept it as one of the tools of the trade, use it as best they can, and move on. They know it's a waste of time to dwell on how quickly it passes.

The time you have belongs to you—unless you give it away or let someone else take it from you. What you do with your allotment is your choice.

We all know school leaders who seem to get more done than others. They don't just do more things in the same amount of time; they seem to know the right things to do and have the will to do them (despite whatever attractive nuisances and seductive distractions may be in their path). How do they do it? It starts by deciding who's boss.

Who Controls Your Time?

"I must govern the clock, not be governed by it."

—Golda Meir

If you want to handle time like your heroes in the profession do, you have to take charge of it. Don't let other people control your calendar or dictate your agenda. Managing time is a matter of choice. As the school leader, you're supposed to do the choosing.

Some administrators show up each day wondering what will happen. Others come to work every morning with a plan for what they want to make happen that day, next week, and next month. That's how effective principals and superintendents get a full 60 seconds out of every minute and get more done in less time.

When administrators let their daily planner, filled in by other people, tell them what to do, they frequently run out of time. When they take charge of their daily activities, however, they often run into time. "Found time" is the reward for aggressive time management.

The first step to shaping time use in your school or organization is to find out how students and staff (including yourself) currently use it. Most educators don't use their time the way they think they do.

The best way to take stock of existing time use is to have people do two things: keep a daily log and conduct a Personal Time-Use Inventory.

Personal Time-Use Inventory

- What routine jobs, meetings, or other functions take up the most time?
- What am I doing that I shouldn't be doing? What would happen if I quit doing it?
- What jobs could be done in a better way or by another person, agency, or organization?
- How do I waste time each day?
- Which students am I not spending enough time with?
- What tasks are taking up more time than they are worth?
- What am I doing that is just plain stupid?
- Which tasks frustrate or anger me?
- Do I have reasons for what I do?
- What activities do I complain about most?
- What's the most useless piece of paperwork I do?
- What tasks make me feel good? What excites me?
- What tasks should I eliminate now? What should I do instead?
- What is the best thing I do each day?
- What things should I definitely be doing that I am not doing now?

Once you are done inventorying, analyze the results, looking for downtime, dumb time, wasted time, and periods of confusion. Pinpoint those functions that are useless, needless, redundant, nonproductive, and counterproductive. Be truthful, realistic, and tough on yourself. Weigh your school's actual time use against how you know you should be—or wish you could be—spending your time and energy.

Knowledge is power, but only if you use it. ("The truth will set you free; but, first, it will tick you off.") Once you've identified where the time goes each school day, week, and year, make changes. Start doing what you're supposed to be doing—not what's easiest to do, what you've always done, what you like to do, or what other people want you to do.

You don't have to become a fanatic about time management; but you're not making the best use of your most valuable resource until you control time more than it controls you.

The gateways to better use of time are setting priorities, sticking to them, and dodging everyday time traps.

Common Time Wasters

Schools are notorious for wasting time. Administrators waste time. Teachers waste time. Students do, too. A moderate amount of innocent inefficiency helps make the school livable; but too much makes it ineffective.

Peak performances by pupils and paid personnel require the economical use of time. Making the most of the limited time available for schooling doesn't just mean doing all the right things as efficiently as possible. It also means avoiding useless, repetitive, and unproductive tasks that steal time from the real work of the school.

If you truly want to accomplish more in less time, then reduce or eliminate time wasters. Following are some common time wasters for school administrators:

- *Dwelling on the past.* For many school leaders, this is the biggest time trap of all. Practicing hindsight and reveling in regret are nonproductive. It's fine to learn from the past. It's wasteful to wallow in it.

- *Waiting.* How much time do you spend waiting for traffic? For appointments? For someone to answer the phone? However much it is, it's too much—if all you do is sit and wait. You'll get a lot more done if you learn to use this downtime to skim reading material, jot down notes, dictate, and take care of other onerous tasks that don't require much thought.

- *Micro-managing.* It's inefficient for you to solve other people's problems. If you don't have enough problems of your own, the school doesn't need you. If you have to oversupervise everything a subordinate does, one of you is useless. Do your job. Let others do theirs. It saves time and works better that way.

- *Marginal meetings and committees that have outlived their usefulness.* Educators are infamous for having too many meetings and committees. They can waste your time and other people's, too. Don't have meetings just because they are on the calendar or form committees just because they have always existed. Make committees and meetings work for you or get rid of them.

- *Too much socializing.* Building relationships, being friendly, and having fun at work are important. But camaraderie alone doesn't get the work done. Being a school leader can't be all socializing, fun, and games. As business guru Harvey McKay says, "That's why they call it work, not summer camp."

- *Perfectionism.* Striving to do everything perfectly is a waste of time. Some projects aren't worth it. Expending high energy on low-yield tasks is a poor use of your most important resource. Give each job its due. No more. That's enough. Move on.

- *Worrying and feeling guilty.* Worry and guilt are self-defeating emotions. They're not tools. They're decoys. Nothing positive was ever accomplished through either one of them.

- *Getting angry.* When others make you angry, they defeat you. Anger doesn't solve problems. It only adds to stress overload. Learn to contain or control your anger (see Steps in Anger Management on the next page).

- *Procrastination.* Delaying action is time mismanagement. Good leaders put off procrastination.

Steps in Anger Management

1. Understand what makes you angry.
2. Know the symptoms of your anger.
3. Know your limits (tolerance level).
4. Avoid anger-provoking situations whenever possible.
5. Do something physical and constructive to dissipate your anger (e.g., jogging, working in the garden).
6. Act out anger in harmless ways (e.g., pound a pillow, write an angry letter and tear it up).

- *Reading the wrong stuff.* Some administrators spend too much time reading everything that crosses their desk. A lot of the material doesn't deserve the attention. Junk mail is just that— junk!

- *Correcting mistakes.* Good time management means doing things right the first time.

- *Frivolous communications.* Technology doesn't always contribute to greater efficiency. Lots of garbage found in faxes and e-mails is a waste of time. Electronic junk mail is just as bad as the U.S. postal variety.

- *Having too many goals.* Some school officials are immobilized by a multiplicity of goals and objectives. When your agenda is everything, nothing gets done.

- *Looking for lost items.* If you can't find it, you can't do it.

- *Walking on eggs.* Time is best served by being straightforward. Beating around the bush just postpones the inevitable. Sparing people's feelings temporarily isn't kindness. It's cowardice. And it wastes time.

- *Paperwork.* Everyone in education is bound up in red tape.

Following are some common classroom time wasters for teachers and students:

- *Classroom interruptions and announcements.* Too many schools have too many interruptions. Students don't learn best in fits and starts. Constantly starting over is a waste of time. Try having your teachers log classroom interruptions for a month. You may be shocked and embarrassed by the results.

- *Pull-outs.* Limited pull-out programs can provide an effective way to meet the needs of special populations. Too many pull-outs, however, only fragment the school day, leaving too little time for necessary whole-group instruction.

- *Unstructured time.* Too much unstructured time (i.e., self-directed study) allows students to drift.

- *Unsupervised study time.* Who doesn't remember wasting time in study hall?

- *Excessive passing time.* If students have time to go to the bathroom, go to their lockers, get a drink, and talk to their friends between classes, there's too much passing time. Hall time isn't productive learning time. Passing time should pass quickly.

- *Dawdling start-ups.* Teachers who are slow in getting started each class period deprive students of entitled learning time. Just a few minutes a day can add up to a couple of lost days of education each year.

- *Early close-downs.* Too many teachers and students close down early before the end of each class period. It's time lost that can't be retrieved. Whatever happened to Yoga Berra's admonition, "It ain't over 'til it's over?" Some schools have had success installing digital clocks to thwart clock-watchers.

- *Purposeless home rooms.* If you don't have a planned activity or a curriculum to cover, home room can be a waste of time.

- *Pepless pep rallies.* If no one is taking attendance and no one is paying attention, pep rallies waste everybody's time at the same time.

- *Noneducational field trips.* One feel-good field trip (just for fun) each year may be worthwhile. Any more than that is a misuse of time and the taxpayer's educational dollars.

- *Discipline disruptions.* Disruptive students take up too much time in today's classrooms. If you want to make better use of every school day, do whatever it takes to improve behavior management.

- *Paperwork.* Like administrators, teachers are drowning in a sea of paperwork. Special education teachers suffer the most.

Just as potholes slow traffic, time wasters slow down productivity in the school. If you want to use the resource of time to everyone's advantage, dodge the potholes.

Setting Priorities: People Versus Paper

Priorities are defined by actions, not by words. What you do tells others what you want them to do. As school leader, how you use your time sets the standard for how teachers and others should spend theirs.

When you want time to count the most, spend it with people, not on paper. How you invest your time sends a message about what's important to the organization. If you make peoplework take precedence over paperwork (see chart below), the message you are sending is "people are what is most important to this organization." If you don't send that message, who will?

Peoplework Versus Paperwork: Which Has the Most Lasting Impact?

Peoplework	Paperwork
Informing	Researching
Instructing	Documenting
Inspiring	Outlining
Meeting	Drafting
Mentoring	Writing
Motivating	Rewriting
Conferencing	Proofreading
Coaching	Correcting
Coaxing	Record keeping
Counseling	Filling out forms
Teaching	Making applications
Persuading	Sorting paper
Influencing	Processing paper
Lobbying	Organizing paper
Listening	Filing paper
Observing	Corresponding
Presenting	Studying
Schmoozing	Reading about work

We all know that paperwork can be appealing and seductive because it is clean, quiet, and safe. Paper doesn't talk back, and you can see definite progress. You even know when you are done. You can't always do that when working with people. Paper doesn't have moods. It's predictable. It stays where you put it—unlike many people, particularly students.

It's easy to see why some administrators choose paper over people; but when they do, they're prostituting a precious resource. Although shuffling paper can keep you busy and make you look and feel productive, it delivers a poor return on your time investment.

Time is better spent with students, staff, parents, school board members, politicians, community leaders, taxpayers, seniors, business representatives, supporters, critics, and ordinary citizens. That's why the most productive principals and superintendents use as much of their time as possible developing relationships, building bridges, managing while walking around (MWWA), opening up communication channels, listening, learning, negotiating, forming coalitions, and building partnerships.

It always pays to direct time and energy toward people because that's where the energy of the organization comes from. People have all the good ideas. People cause the problems; but they also create the solutions. People produce results. They do all the dreaming; and they also do the actual work.

Time is a finite resource. To spend it wisely, you never go wrong making people your priority. It's a much better use of time to leave a legacy of leading people, than merely a paper trail, no matter how neat and complete.

If you need further evidence that doing peoplework is the right choice, just ask yourself, "How many great leaders do I know who prefer paperwork?" Odds are the count is zero. What does that tell you about priorities?

When and How to Say "No" and Make It Stick

Making good use of school time demands staying focused on big-ticket items (priorities) and avoiding time traps. One of the best tools for accomplishing both is the simple word *no*. You should probably be using it more.

Some administrators are reluctant to say "no" because they think it's a negative response and that using it makes them come across as a negative leader. They're wrong. *No* isn't always negative. Sometimes, it's the most positive response you can make. Sometimes, it's the only right response.

Saying "no" is just another way to set priorities. It's a time-saver. Turning down an added task or responsibility, a new activity, and another invitation are the easiest, quickest, and simplest ways to clear your calendar of nuisance or needless time demands.

You know it's the right time to say "no" when:

- You already have too many irons in the fire (when your plate is full, don't take any more helpings).

- You hate the activity (if you detest the task, you won't do a good job anyway—why bother?).

- The project is a loser (if it's a bad idea, don't waste your time prolonging the agony).

- You have no passion for the task (lack of enthusiasm and lackluster performances go together—if you have no excitement for the project, let someone else do it).

- There is no growth opportunity (if you are going to take on something new, make it something challenging and worthwhile).

- The timing is wrong (wasting time on a project whose time has not yet come is like pouring sand down the proverbial rat hole—don't even think about it).

- The job is not worth the effort (whenever a project promises a low yield for a high amount of effort, it's a lose-lose situation—back off).

- There's a better way to do it (why waste your time on something that's second best?).

- Someone else can do it better, faster, or easier (part of the efficient and effective use of time is giving the right job to the right person).

- It's a project in name only, designed for the sake of appearance (if a task is only cosmetic, you can find better uses for your time).

- It doesn't feel right (trust your instincts and intuition—if your gut says "No," you should say "No.").

When "No" is obviously the right answer, the trick is not just to say it but to make it stick. The following work for many busy leaders who have mastered the art of refusal:

1. Be firm and clear. Don't turn your response into a guessing game. Don't waffle. Many people are eager to interpret "No, but—" or "Maybe" as a "Yes." You can't say "no" by hint or innuendo. Spit it out. It will save time and misunderstanding.

2. Give your reason(s) for your response without guilt or apology. Don't debate your decision. Move on.

3. Be willing to repeat your response as often as it takes.

Saying "no" to nonsense leaves more time to say "yes" to what's worthwhile. Using the word *no* isn't just a convenience; it's the surest, fastest way to simplify your life and relieve stress at the same time. Saying "no" is a work-smarter technique and a survival skill for any administrator who wants to pack every minute with productive activity. That's you, isn't it?

How the Best Leaders Spend 1,440 Minutes a Day

The best leaders in education (or any field) are also the best users of time. They don't actually do more things in a given time period than others; but they do different things.

Although they have the same amount of time as the rest of us, effective leaders find time, make time, or take time to do what matters most. Here's how some of the most successful school administrators report using their 1,440 minutes each day:

- Spending time planning how to spend time
- Doing what's most important to their job first
- Doing what they do best (building on strengths)
- Planning, dreaming, and envisioning what's possible
- Practicing anticipatory thinking (spotting trends and problems before they materialize)
- Decision making, problem solving, and risk taking
- Teaching, coaching, instructing, and inspiring

- Changing things that need to be changed
- Dealing with setbacks through renewed effort
- Getting the most out of others
- Nurturing the culture of the organization
- Concentrating on image control rather than damage control
- Modeling integrity, authenticity, and ethical behavior
- Conserving, stretching, and renewing resources
- Making time for self-renewal, family, fun, friends, community service, and spirituality.

Wow! Does that sound like your day?

The average administrator would like to spend more time doing the things on this list, but always seems to be too busy putting out brush fires, reacting to crises, and taking care of day-to-day administrivia. How do successful school leaders ever have time to truly lead the organization, instead of just managing its routine operations? It's not a mystery. It's mostly a matter of discipline, focus, and hard work.

The time to lead is there for anyone willing to delegate, prioritize, follow up, follow through, be organized, tackle problems sooner rather than later, and use their moods and biological clock to their advantage. Using these time stretchers to squeeze every ounce of productivity out of every hour of the day isn't magic. It's a decision.

When you spend it in the right way, there's plenty of time to go around. If you've read this far, that should be no surprise. What's true of time is true of all the resources of the school. When you apply the principles of fiscal fitness, you'll find that you already have enough. Your school can become astonishingly good with just what you have now.

Practical Ways to Reduce Paperwork

Teachers and administrators agree. There's too much paperwork. And it's getting worse!

Rather than producing a paperless office or school as predicted, modern technology has proliferated the demand for information. Worse yet, everyone wants a hard copy of everything.

Coupled with the outpourings of faxes and e-mails, mushrooming regulations and rampant paranoia about the need to document everything have conspired to multiply paperwork for school personnel at all levels. Schools today are being buried in an avalanche of paper.

It's now entirely possible for educators to work virtually full-time on paperwork. Some administrators actually do. Some teachers do, too. (Just check with the chair of your special education department.)

Concerned school leaders can't address the issue of wasted time without considering how to tame the paper tiger. Anything that reduces paperwork releases time for real work with real teachers and kids.

Of course, the best way to reduce paperwork is simply to produce and request less. It has to start at the top. If the principal or superintendent demands less paper, everyone else can follow suit.

If you want to truly maximize teaching and learning time in your school, lead the charge to minimize paper mania and manage the paper flow throughout the organization. This may be the single most important contribution you can make to improving time use.

Practical ways to lighten the paper load in any school include the following:

- Crack down on the overuse of worksheets for students.
- Put one person in charge of access to fax machines and copiers and install key access to all copy machines.
- Remind everyone that the wastebasket is a timesaving device.
- Don't just shuffle paper. Deal with it. Handle paper only once.
- Learn to skim and scan what you read. Read only what you need to read. Skip unnecessary details. Often, reading the introduction, conclusion, and recommendations is enough.
- Challenge everyone in the organization to continually ask, "Is this form [letter, memo, report, record, etc.] really necessary?"
- Model clear, concise writing. You may educate your staff to write economically.
- "Junk" junk mail.
- Delegate your paper load. Have someone else screen your mail, "ghost write," and "ghost read" for you when necessary.

- Simplify correspondence by developing a battery of form letters.
- Use old reports as models for new ones. Don't reinvent the wheel every time a report is due.
- Eliminate cover letters that don't add any substantive content. (Most cover letters just say, "I'm sending . . ." or "Here it is . . . ")
- Enforce a strict "need to know" criteria for sending copies to secondary sources.
- Make one report serve dual purposes.
- Be informal with your written responses (e.g., use sticky notes or response cards or write responses in the margin or at the bottom of original correspondence).
- Let the people who are really good at paperwork do it.

Any school can look good on paper. The best schools, however, downplay paperwork and concentrate instead on the real world of working with kids. That's the very best use of time.

Other Ways to Work Smarter, Save Time, and Do More

Making maximum use of time takes time. The very best school leaders have the time because they know how to cut corners, combine tasks, streamline procedures, sidestep time traps, and work smarter than most people. They're not born with this knowledge. They learn it. You can, too.

Following are more work-smarter strategies and techniques that any administrator can use to make more time available for teaching and learning:

- Use—don't abuse—electronic messages. Don't copy every message to everybody in the organization. Think before you write, not as you write.
- Focus on major responsibilities. For lesser tasks, delegate and deputize as much as possible.
- Confine e-mail to in-house messages, except for emergencies.
- Set and enforce deadlines.

- Stress goal setting. Keep major goals visible at all times.
- Establish some quiet time every day. (Call a time out on electronic messages. Only face-to-face interaction allowed.)
- Categorize tasks. Batch everything you want or need to do in like groups.
- Use aides and secretaries as buffers.
- Minimize classroom interruptions and intrusions.
- Let your good habits (punctuality, precise record keeping, etc.) work for you.
- Plan for interruptions.
- Do the most urgent and important tasks first.
- Start and end meetings on time.
- Buffer teachers and other staff members from intrusive vendors.
- Learn when to talk, when to listen, and when to work.
- Schedule specific times to respond to correspondence, answer calls, check mail, and see people. Block out time for family and for yourself as well.
- Organize your desk to funnel attention to priority projects.
- Substitute a "door ajar" policy for the customary open-door policy.
- Reward yourself for working smarter.

Even when you can't work any longer, harder, or faster, you can still work smarter. There's never a shortage of time when you are creative enough to keep coming up with better ways of doing things. You can't beat time, but sometimes you can outsmart it.

Tips on More Efficient Scheduling of the School Day and the School Year

Like most resources, time can be manipulated to your advantage. That's why schools have an annual calendar and a master schedule. How you schedule people, events, and activities goes a long way in determining how efficiently you use your time with students.

Scheduling the school year and the school day are not idle exercises in logistics. They are a means of arranging time to meet your needs, rather than adjusting your needs to fit time demands. The master student schedule and the annual calendar are two of the school's most valuable tools for managing time to create maximum opportunities for instructional use.

The purpose of the master schedule is to provide students with the widest possible range of opportunities to build individual academic programs that meet their specific needs. It is a primary instrument for manipulating school time to promote optimum learning and productivity.

Because time can be carved up in many ways, school leaders need to examine all options for making every minute count for learning. The easiest variables to manipulate are the following: (a) length of class periods, (b) the number of periods per day, (c) the length and timing of lunch periods, and (d) the time before and after school, which can be a means of offering optional courses to interested students.

Master schedules don't come in one size that fits all. There are myriad ways of putting the pieces together. To avoid being locked in by what has always been, it is important to remember that almost any schedule is possible and almost any schedule is workable if the staff believes in it and is committed to its implementation.

The trick is to determine what kind of daily time arrangement best suits the school's individual situation, provides the greatest possible amount of instructional time, and facilitates the creativity and flexibility that the staff needs to be fully productive.

Some of the most popular alternatives to traditional scheduling include the following:

- Block scheduling (lengthening periods and reducing the number of classes per day)
- Schedules within a schedule (creating specialized schedules within the regular schedule to accommodate diverse populations)
- Split scheduling (having two groups attend at alternate times)
- Trimester plans
- Year-round school
- Extended school day
- Extended summer school

- Flexible entry and exit
- Built-in remediation sessions during the school day

The amount of school time available each day is relatively static; but its use can be as flexible as the staff's creativity permits. You can't stretch time; you can twist it to serve your purposes.

For example, when Anoka (Minnesota) High School was faced with accommodating 3,000 pupils in a facility designed for only 2,000, the school adopted a schedule whereby students could work with community business partners during the regular school day and receive three credits, then attend core classes from 3 to 6 p.m. In Anoka and elsewhere, the operable criteria for a master schedule is "whatever works best."

In addition to the time scheduled for formal classes, it also pays to consider better ways to use unscheduled time during the school day. How students and staff spend their time outside of class can have a lot to do with the school's overall productivity.

Learning doesn't have to be confined to formal class periods. There are a lot of ways to help students learn between, before, and after regular classes and during other unscheduled periods. These bits and pieces of time shouldn't just be lost or go unnoticed. They can provide newfound opportunities to increase the amount of learning time each day through the use of independent or self-directed study, learning kiosks, or optional minicourses.

Just as the master schedule structures the use of time on a daily basis, the school calendar provides a blueprint for how the school uses its time over the entire year.

The annual calendar is the school's guide to organizing and scheduling key events and activities to make the most efficient use of the total year. Care spent in mapping out school activities on a yearlong basis saves time and frustration later in resolving conflicts, rescheduling events, and squeezing in last-minute items. A well-organized school calendar helps everyone plan better for the entire year.

The following guidelines can help ensure a functional yearlong calendar adaptable to any school situation:

1. The calendar should promote optimal learning opportunities for all students.
2. The calendar must conform to all existing state laws and employee contracts.

3. The calendar should be as family friendly as possible.

4. The calendar should be respectful of religious and ethnic holidays.

5. The calendar should respect local scheduling traditions, such as "church night," community celebrations, political caucus nights, town meetings, and so on.

6. Marking (grading) periods should be balanced through the year.

7. The calendar should mesh with those of other schools and organizations.

8. Care should be taken to avoid unduly chopping up the school year. The goal is to schedule as much uninterrupted instructional time as possible.

9. Important events should not be scheduled immediately before or after holidays or vacation periods.

10. The calendar should be planned so that the school doesn't end up competing with itself (i.e., having two or more major activities scheduled at the same time).

11. Parent-teacher conferences should be scheduled at the convenience of the parents, not the teachers.

12. The calendar should facilitate the economical use of transportation services as much as possible.

A carefully sequenced school calendar is always the first step toward effectively managing limited school time over the course of an entire year.

Once the annual calendar and the daily master schedule are in place, it's up to the staff to use these tools to make the most of all the time that has been so carefully planned. Ultimately, effective time management simply boils down to planning the work and working the plan.

Start Time: Is Later Better?

Fiscal fitness is a learning process. We are continuously finding new and better ways to make the most of our most essential resources—including time. Rethinking school starting times for teenagers is one of the best recent examples.

Many secondary schools across the nation have traditionally begun around 7:15 a.m. to 7:45 a.m. That's too early, according to a growing number of physicians and sleep experts.

The rapidly emerging consensus of sleep researchers is that U.S. teens aren't getting enough sleep and academic performance is suffering as a result. As explained by Michele Kipke, director of the National Academy of Science's Board on Children, Youth, and Families, "Sleep experts feel really strongly that high school timings are out of sync with the natural circadian rhythms of adolescents."

Increasingly, scientists now agree that adolescents need an average of nine hours of sleep nightly to satisfy their biological needs. Most are getting far less. How many of your teachers have you heard complain about kids sleeping in class?

Trying to teach students who are too tired to learn is a waste of time. If your students' biological clocks and natural metabolism aren't ready for calculus (or any other subject) at 7:30 a.m., starting later may enable your teachers to teach more, better, and faster in the same amount of time. They should give out medals for something like that.

Because of recent findings, many high schools (and some middle schools) around the country are reconsidering their start times. Some have already pushed back their beginning time in hopes of becoming more efficient, effective, and productive. Starting later may be one more way you can use time to everyone's advantage.

How to Have Fewer Interruptions and More Time on Task

"The fragmentation of the classroom is killing teachers and schools."

—Fifth-grade teacher

If you're serious about making better use of time and want a good place to start, take a look at the number of classroom interruptions in your school.

Do your students have too much downtime or fragmented time and too little time on task? Are there too many noninstructional intrusions on what's supposed to be instructional time? Do your teachers joke about installing revolving doors on their classrooms? Are teachers and parents frustrated by the frequent interruption of the school day and the school year? If yours is like most schools, the answer is a resounding "yes" to all of the above.

Here's how bad the problem is nationwide:

- National studies reveal that out of the 1,770 hours in a typical school year, many schools actually spend only about 500 on real learning activities.

- Some urban classrooms have as many as 16 or more different programs pulling kids out of class during the year.

- Experts claim that many classrooms are interrupted as much as 125 times per week.

- Some schools use as little as one-third of their time for actual academic learning. (If schools could increase this merely to 50%, they would gain weeks of extra learning time without expending any significant amounts of money.)

Interruptions can be distracting, wasteful, and nonproductive. Is it happening in your school?

Cutting down on unnecessary intrusions seems like a small step toward greater efficiency and better use of time resources, but it is a step. That's what all progress is made up of.

Adding days to the school year can cost thousands—maybe millions—of dollars. Tightening up on interruptions can accomplish much of the same thing at almost no cost. A growing number of schools think it's worthwhile.

Following are the kinds of remedies being tried by some of your colleagues (your staff can probably think of many more):

- Conduct an inventory of interruptions. Identify which programs are competing with core academic work. Ask students, teachers, and parents about the value of today's proliferation of intrusions.

- Lobby for fewer fire drills. These drills are important safety precautions, but are monthly simulations essential during every year of a child's schooling?

- Batch student birthdays together for once-a-month classroom celebrations instead of holding numerous individual celebrations throughout the month.

- Limit the number of field trips.
- Restrict the number of classroom visitors.
- Consider holding elementary band and orchestra classes before or after the regular school day. (It works for athletics.)
- Let teachers read building announcements at their convenience, rather than having the principal interrupt at his or her convenience from the front office.
- Challenge the PTA and booster clubs to find ways to minimize the amount of teacher time required to collect or account for money from fundraisers.
- Replace all those staff development "released days" during the year with a weeklong instructional academy at the end of the year.

Reducing interruptions increases time on task, which improves student and staff productivity. That's what school boards live for.

Many intrusions are beyond the teachers' control, but not beyond the control of the administration. That's you. Any school can cut down on classroom interruptions and boost effective learning time. Why not make it your school?

This chapter has tried to show that time is simply another resource for the school. It should be treated as one. Being a good steward of time is as important as being a good money manager.

No responsible administrator would spend money or deploy personnel without careful forethought. Time use deserves the same attention. Think about it.

7

More Ways to Save Time and Money

Fiscal fitness can be a gift that keeps on giving. Economies have a way of begetting more of the same. Once a school staff acquires the habit of thinking about maximizing all available and existing resources, new possibilities for saving and streamlining seem to surface automatically. Serendipity is often the mother of efficiency.

This chapter is packed with ways that schools are making resources go further. These ideas are just starter suggestions, meant to trigger more and better money-saving and time-saving opportunities and applications. It can work that way in your school. All you have to do is be open to inspiration.

Building-Level Economies You Can Implement Today

Despite what some school boards and superintendents may think, the best things in education usually start at the building level. That includes the best ways to stretch resources and do more with less.

You don't have to wait for fiscal fitness to originate in the front office. Individual schools can lead the way in cutting costs and eliminating waste just as independent small businesses often do in the private sector.

Due to the nature of your student population or other circumstances, you may not have the top test scores or the winningest sports teams in the district. But you can have the best record of resource management. Your school can get more out of its time, money, and personnel than all the rest. You can set the pace for fiscal fitness.

It starts by understanding that even little savings add up. Effective managers never thumb their nose at small economies. They just keep piling up new efficiencies, building on existing budget stretchers, and looking for more and better ways to reduce waste until "suddenly" they have amassed eye-popping savings.

To get started immediately, following are a dozen strategies that schools large and small are using to achieve extraordinary results. Some of these measures are small steps. Others are far-reaching. None are very fancy. They don't have to be. But they all add up. You can put them to work in your school today or use them to generate even better ideas for implementation in your own situation now or later.

1. Turn off the lights. Shutting down lights when classrooms are not in use can produce amazing savings. Sometimes fiscal fitness is just the click of a switch away. Many schools have been able to trim electric bills as much as 15% just by turning down or turning off unneeded lights throughout the building.

2. Raise the ceiling for hiring classroom aides. Even just adding two or three pupils to the ceiling can save the cost of a full-time position across the entire building. Is it worth it? You'll have to decide.

3. Wage war on classroom intrusions and pull-out program interruptions (see Chapter 6 for suggestions). In some schools, teachers complain that they "spend five minutes of every hour teaching and the rest of the time sending kids out for Ritalin." Don't let that happen on your watch.

4. Show your teachers how they can help the school save money and save on their income tax at the same time. Any expense that helps your faculty members improve their teaching or is used in their work can usually be deducted from money owed the IRS. These expenses can include book purchases, magazine subscriptions, zoo memberships, student supplies, and other teaching materials and equipment—as long as they are used exclusively for teaching.

All of these purchases can be used to assist the school. That makes it easy for teachers to help out and help themselves as well. Some schools even go so far as to bring in a local tax accountant to conduct employee workshops on what's deductible and what's not.

Expecting teachers to spend their own money on school supplies may not be fair, but it happens in every school every day. You might as well make it organized and systematic so that it can be of the greatest benefit to the school and to the individual teachers who take money out of their own pockets.

5. Reduce overtime. Working overtime can become a habit, even an epidemic, among clerical and maintenance personnel. If employees start counting on overtime pay and scaling their lifestyle accordingly, you're either understaffed or you're getting ripped off.

Monitor overtime closely. If there are questions or problems, clean up your procedures. It may be necessary to personally approve or authorize all after-hours work until expenditures are under control.

No school should have to pay time-and-a-half wages for regular work on a regular basis. It's wasteful and expensive. You don't need it.

6. Reduce the cost of doing business. In some schools and school systems, it costs as much or more to process a purchase than the cost of the purchase itself (e.g., a $5.00 purchase can cost as much as $100 in labor costs to process). That may not be malfeasance, but it is serious waste and extravagance.

Try issuing credit cards to teachers and other appropriate staff members for use at approved stores for approved supplies. It saves time. It saves money. And it makes employees feel empowered. You can't do much better than that.

7. Assign all special education paperwork to clerical workers. It has saved some school districts as much as $100,000 a year.

8. Streamline the keeping of students' records. One of the biggest sources of paperwork overwork for schools is the system for keeping students' records. Over the years, pupil folders often become bloated with obsolete permission slips, outdated work samples, casual teacher notations, and other "junk records."

Efficiency-minded schools save time, effort, paper, space, and money by purging all student files of nonessential materials on a regular basis. Make it a point to clean out the records of all transfer students within 3 days. Try it. You'll like it.

9. Turn over costly extracurricular club activities (e.g., camera club, environmental club, chess club, ski club) to the district's community education department. Most community education pro-

grams are self-supporting and can continue to offer these activities to students on a fee basis.

10. Boost school lunch revenues by enforcing an accurate portion control system. Guesswork, inconsistency, or favoritism in dishing up food servings has no place in the school lunch line.

11. Don't be too proud to scrounge for free stuff. Work with your staff to "scavenge" for discarded office supplies that would be usable classroom materials for students. You might be surprised by how many businesses throw away better stuff than some schools buy in the first place.

12. Consider becoming an ISO 9000-certified school. ISO 9000, sponsored by the International Organization for Standardization, is a nuts-and-bolts business tool used to enforce efficiency and discipline on unwieldy systems. It involves a third-party audit of operations and is used extensively by businesses worldwide to verify consistency. ISO 9000 certification serves as a seal of approval indicating that the organization lives up to its word.

Some school administrators are now exploring use of the ISO 9000 certification process as a tool for realizing fiscal fitness in the public sector. The Lancaster (Pennsylvania) Schools were among the first in the nation to adopt the program in 1998.

Take a look. This just might be your school's ticket to greater efficiency and productivity.

Effecting these or any other building-level economies isn't intended as a means of giving kids less. It's really an exercise in identifying compromises and trade-offs in order to serve students better. That's what schools are supposed to do.

Tips on Efficient Plant Management

Because educational organizations are labor intensive, the most painless way to reduce costs or waste is through better management of the nonhuman resources of the school. The best place to start is often with the physical plant itself. Whatever can be saved through more efficient plant management can be applied to much-needed personnel costs.

Although most school administrators aren't maintenance engineers or energy experts, they are ultimately responsible for respecting and protecting the physical plant of the school and getting the most out of all electrical, mechanical, and other systems throughout the facility. As the chief steward of the school's buildings, grounds, and other facilities, you have specific responsibilities for plant supervision and management.

School Administrator's Responsibilities for Plant Management

- Ensuring the safety of all facilities
- Preserving and maintaining the infrastructure of the school
- Meeting the standards and requirements of all building codes.
- Establishing a systematic program of preventive maintenance
- Maintaining a regular schedule for monitoring and inspecting all facilities, equipment, and mechanical systems
- Adapting facilities to changing needs
- Promoting energy efficiency wherever possible
- Recommending necessary and desirable capital improvements
- Upgrading facilities as new and better products become available
- Maintaining and enhancing (where possible) the aesthetic appearance of the physical plant
- Engendering a sense of pride and ownership of the school's facilities on the part of students and the community

---

The two biggest steps that building leaders can take to save costs in plant operation are to establish an aggressive program of preventive maintenance and to increase energy efficiency and conservation through installation of computerized energy management and other operating systems.

Effective administrators are fanatics about preventive maintenance. Every school's motto should be: "Prepare and prevent—not repair and repent." The life span of essential operating systems can be stretched literally by years, sometimes decades, through proper use, attentive care, and preventive maintenance. It's impossible to overemphasize these measures.

The best means of staying ahead of facility decay and system deterioration are to insist on high standards of cleanliness throughout the physical plant, to conduct frequent checks on all operating systems, to use tickler files to avoid neglecting or forgetting important maintenance work, to scrupulously follow all manufacturers' recommendations for upkeep, to follow up on the findings of all Occupational Safety and Health Administration and other inspections, and to call on outside experts (architects, engineers, building inspectors) to perform thorough plant assessments on a regular basis (every 2 to 5 years).

The second major part of being a good steward of the physical plant is to champion energy efficiency. Schools are notorious energy sieves. This is particularly true of secondary schools where students have a propensity for turning on lights and leaving them burning, leaving doors open or ajar, and opening and closing windows.

That's why all school leaders have to be increasingly energy sensitive. Taking the lead in reducing energy costs and consumption pays big dividends because (a) it curtails operating costs, (b) it models environmental protection, (c) it sends the right message to kids about conserving resources, and (d) it creates positive public relations throughout the community.

Where energy efficiency is a problem or concern, more and more schools are finding the answer in automatic systems for monitoring and controlling energy equipment. Fortunately, it is often possible to apply for energy grants or other government matching funds to purchase and install these systems.

Use of automated equipment can produce both energy and dollar savings. Most administrators are astonished at the amount of consumption reduction and cost savings that result from converting to automated energy management and monitoring systems.

Of course, there are a lot of other ways to promote plant efficiency besides preventive maintenance and computerized energy systems. Following are a few of the best and easiest to implement:

- Retrofit the lighting. Replace all incandescent bulbs and old fluorescence with new compact fluorescent lighting.

- Turn thermostats up (or down) as appropriate for conditions. Installing programmable thermostats can save even more.

Some schools have experienced savings of 1% on heating bills for every day they set back thermostats during downtime.

- Insist on using the most advanced cleaning supplies and equipment.

- Upgrade boilers. Schedule regular professional maintenance checks for all boilers including checks on air pressure, burners and heat exchanges, and sediment scales and other build-up inside the units.

- Modernize all exterior windows.

- Reduce the water flow in urinals.

- Be aggressive about recycling. Reusing materials and supplies is beneficial economically and environmentally.

- Install low-flow shower heads.

- Fix leaky faucets and fountains as quickly as possible. A single drip per second can add up to 2,400 of wasted gallons of water in a year's time.

- Landscape for conservation. You can lower energy bills by strategically planting trees and shrubs to channel cool breezes in summer and reduce cold drafts in winter. It's not unheard of to cut up to 25% in air conditioning costs this way. (And you thought that shrubbery was just for aesthetics.)

- Don't put off making needed facility improvements. Most save money in the long run.

- Join with other governmental agencies to negotiate lower electrical rates from your local utility company. You may be shocked by how easy it is.

Although it is important for administrators to take the lead in promoting the efficient use of the school's physical plant and operating systems, it can be overdone. Don't get carried to extremes or fall prey to false economies (e.g., skimping on preventive maintenance). Two of the biggest mistakes school officials often make in plant management are the following:

1. Turning off air exchanges to save energy costs. This can be detrimental (even dangerous) to the indoor air quality of the school. (Students can't learn when every day is a bad air day.)

2. Trying to achieve economies of scale by building larger and larger schools. When it comes to learning, bigger isn't always better. Any school enrolling more than 800 to 1,000 pupils runs the risk of experiencing lower achievement and increased student alienation. It's not worth it.

Avoiding such false economies and still realizing optimum cost-effectiveness in plant operations should be a key component of every administrator's fiscal fitness plan. Every dollar saved in managing nonhuman resources can be invested in "people resources," which really pay the biggest dividends for kids in the long run.

Make the Most of Technology to Save Time and Money

The scramble to keep up with the latest technologies is one of the main reasons that school budgets everywhere are being stretched beyond the limit.

Technology doesn't come cheap. Computers are expensive. So are big-screen televisions, VCRs, stereos, camcorders, fax machines, color copiers, and all the other paraphernalia that make up modern technology. Not only does all of this technology cost a lot but much of it becomes obsolete almost overnight.

Just trying to stay abreast of the changes to give kids useful technological tools and skills is consuming a disproportionate share of most schools' financial resources.

Worse yet, if misused or abused, today's technologies can actually create waste, contribute to communication gridlock and overload, undermine productivity, and distract from the primary purpose of the organization. (But that's the subject of another book.)

The good news is that the technology that depletes school resources can also be used to conserve and stretch resources and allow the school to do more with less.

Most schools have just scratched the surface in using technology to enhance resource management. Yours is no exception. The potential for harnessing technology to boost school efficiency and productivity goes off the charts.

If you are not currently putting state-of-the-art technology to work for the following,

- Internet learning
- Independent research
- Desktop publishing
- Word processing
- Spreadsheet accounting
- Student scheduling and energy monitoring and management
- School bus routing using digitized maps
- Processing of work orders
- Computerized substitute calling

you should be. But that's not enough!

Technology is the management tool of the 21st century. School officials who don't take maximum advantage of today's and tomorrow's technology are forfeiting their claim to leadership.

Superintendents and principals don't have to know everything about technology and how it works, but they should know what is available and what is possible.

If you don't have a cadre of computer wizards and other "techies" on the payroll, you are unfairly handicapping your school's capability to achieve cost-effectiveness, optimum efficiency, and maximum productivity.

Likewise, if you allow technology costs to run amuck, they will devour your school's resources. Used effectively, however, technology can be your greatest weapon against waste.

Schools can't just keep hiring more and more people at higher and higher salaries to get the job done. School leaders have to find a way to live within their means. Technology is the key. Use it. There just isn't any better way to save time and money.

Save Money on Substitute Teachers

It's not just technology costs that are pushing school budgets over the edge. In many schools, personnel expenses are also becoming budget-busters. One growing area of concern is the escalating costs of substitute teachers.

Too many schools use too many subs. It's not uncommon for schools to have a dozen or more subs every day of the year. Occasionally, some schools have more substitute teachers in the building than regular teachers. Not only is the presence of this many subs educationally detrimental but it can also be economically damaging.

Any time you bring a substitute teacher into the classroom, you are paying two people to do the same job. It doesn't take an economics major to figure out that this is not a good deal.

Parents and students don't like too many substitutes. You shouldn't either. Every time your substitute teacher costs increase, your discretionary dollars shrink.

Of course, a certain amount of absenteeism requiring the use of substitutes is inevitable. In some schools, however, excessive or chronic absenteeism is a major problem—and a major expense. A few schools even develop an "absenteeism culture" where attendance is taken lightly and almost any excuse for missing work is eagerly embraced by staff members. This level of absenteeism is both a symptom and a cause of an unhealthy work environment. If this is the situation in your school, you have more serious problems than high sub costs.

Even where absence rates are average, the costs are high. The only real way to significantly reduce expenditures for substitutes is to reduce teacher absences. The six most successful strategies for improving teacher attendance (and diminishing the need for substitutes) are the following:

1. Initiating accurate record keeping and documentation of absences. The first step toward improving employee attendance is always gathering accurate data.
2. Monitoring absenteeism, recording trends, identifying chronic problem areas (see Common Patterns of Teacher Absence below), and concentrating on the offending employees.

Common Patterns of Teacher Absence

- The more contractual leave days available, the more days are likely to be used.
- There are more absences by employees who live long distances from the school.
- Attendance is usually highest on paydays.
- Mondays tend to be bad days for attendance.
- Frequently, absentee rates increase as retirement approaches.

Frequent Causes of Teacher Attendance Problems

- Low morale
- Mental or emotional problems (including substance abuse)
- Substandard working conditions (including extreme discipline problems and incidents of school violence)
- Misunderstandings of contractual leave provisions
- Inflexible schedules
- Poor supervision (lack of leadership)

---

3. Requiring personnel to report absences personally and directly to their immediate supervisor rather than to an automated recording or code-a-phone device. This makes more work for supervisors, but it reduces absences every time.

4. Making a big deal out of attendance. (The first step to success is to show up.) Model regular and consistent attendance and expect others to do the same.

5. Stressing personal fitness, health, and wellness. Some schools have successfully improved faculty health and attendance by sponsoring smoking-cessation clinics, scheduling on-site diet support group meetings, providing exercise equipment in the teachers' lounge, and negotiating special rates for teachers at local health and fitness clubs.

6. Following the practical "dos and don'ts" on the next page.

When you've taken these steps and others and have done all you can do to improve teacher attendance, you're still not done trying to save money on subs. The following measures can often reduce substitute costs even further:

- Get other staff members to cover for absences of short duration. It's not even heresy for the administrator-in-charge to take over a class for a few hours.

- Find ways to interrupt (break up) a teacher's extended absence by filling in with a regular staff member for a day or two to avoid paying long-term sub rates, which are usually considerably higher than the regular daily rate of pay.

Dos and Don'ts of Attendance Improvement

Do	*Don't*
Publicize absenteeism trends and profiles and show the costs involved.	Ignore absences.
Provide each teacher with a printout of his or her attendance record annually.	Neglect to stress the importance of attendance in preemployment interviews.
Urge teachers to save personal leave days for true emergencies or significant family events.	Maintain inadequate or inaccurate records.
Send get-well cards, visit staff members who are ill, and welcome returning teachers following each absence.	Omit attendance as a factor in professional performance reviews.
As an attendance incentive, allocate funds saved from reduced sub costs for building use.	Penalize teachers with good attendance by requiring them to cover for absent colleagues.
Consider paying for unused sick leave.	Encourage teachers to come to school sick. It usually results in more prolonged absences.
Recognize outstanding attendance records.	

- Combine less-than-full-day sub requests so that all substitutes have full-day assignments. Partial-day subs often earn a full day's pay even though they don't work that long.
- Use retired teachers or nonlicensed personnel as subs (where permitted). Their pay rates are often less than active, fully licensed substitutes.

Money spent on substitute teachers does nothing to improve the quality of teaching and learning in the school. Don't just accept high sub costs. Do something about them. It's the fiscal fitness thing to do.

Eighty-Eight More School-Tested Time and Money Savers

When school staff members are united and get serious about cutting costs, eliminating waste, and channeling resources where they really belong, they can make it happen. It's a lot easier, however, when they have examples of how other faculties go about it.

If your staff's creative pump needs priming, the following real-world strategies and suggestions may help get you started. Some are suited for building-level efforts. Others are designed for district-level implementation. They all are working somewhere. And they're free for the taking. Feel free to borrow or build on them as needed.

1. Buy in bulk.
2. Consolidate transportation routes.
3. Eliminate job duplication.
4. Join a co-op to be eligible for discounts on everything from crayons to computers—even telephone service.
5. Don't fill vacancies immediately. Using subs or temps for a while can reduce costs by as much as 22%.
6. Hire health aides instead of school nurses.
7. Reduce inventories and implement "just in time" ordering procedures. (It works in business all the time.)
8. Salvage and reuse fixtures and other equipment from renovated schools.
9. Enter into joint purchasing agreements with the city, county, and other school districts.
10. Pay secondary teachers to teach a sixth class rather than hiring new personnel and paying for additional benefits.
11. Limit field trips.
12. Reduce dues, memberships, and subscriptions.
13. Turn to hometown talent before bringing in an outside consultant.
14. Check out government supply sources. They're usually cheaper.
15. Offer early retirement incentives.
16. Consider buying used buses, computers, and so on.

17. Use portable classrooms instead of building new ones.

18. Maximize earned interest on investments.

19. Cut travel costs.

20. Reduce the size of the summer paint crew.

21. Settle for fewer district administrators and/or support staff.

22. Use as long a grace period for paying bills as vendors and suppliers will allow. The longer you can keep your money the better.

23. Hire a good business manager. It's the single most important thing you can do to ensure fiscal fitness.

24. Shop around for better deals. Take bids even if you don't have to. You'll get cheaper supplies.

25. Adopt a "design-build" construction model by using the same contractor as both architect and builder.

26. Consolidate schools with low enrollments.

27. Cut back on or cut out professional and sabbatical leaves.

28. Permit principals more flexibility in handling accounts. Let them exercise the power of trade-offs.

29. Assign warehouse and print shop employees to other tasks during off-peak periods.

30. Hire personnel who have less experience and less training.

31. Share conference and convention registrations with other schools.

32. Dump periodicals that are no longer popular with students and/or staff.

33. Save postage by continually updating and trimming mailing lists.

34. Make the food service program self-supporting.

35. Pair schools for transportation by staggering starting times.

36. Watch for federal and state government surplus sales.

37. Recycle white paper (regular and computer). Paper companies will often buy it at a good price.

38. Request suggestions from manufacturers and vendors on how to save on maintenance, operation, and repair costs.

39. Renegotiate a better deal with your vending machine owner.

Food Service Tips

- Develop a marketing plan, including a new menu and a variety of promotional activities and events.
- Use plastic film wrap instead of foil wrap.
- Buy 1% milk instead of 2%.
- Buy a cheese-grating machine. (One district eliminated a full-time food service position this way.)
- Centralize food preparation and downsize kitchens in satellite centers.
- Hold inventory at the lowest possible level.
- Cut down waste.
- Combine government commodity food with other ingredients.
- Build up supplemental sales. The goal should be to sell every student at least one food item every day.

---

40. Rent out vacant space (if you have it).

41. Cut out royalties for high-priced theater productions. Stage only plays old enough to be public domain.

42. Expand your list of qualified suppliers to include out-of-state vendors. You never know where you will find the best bargains.

43. Use certified mail rather than sending telegrams.

44. Reduce clerical staff by using temps or students during peak periods.

45. Cut your own post cards from stock and meter them for mailing.

46. Make everyone more time conscious and sensitive by scheduling meetings at odd times (e.g., 8:57 a.m.).

47. Post all of the school's forms on a display board and ask staff members to suggest ways to streamline, consolidate, or eliminate.

48. Take the state to court. Challenge the state's educational funding formula (sue the state) to win more adequate and equitable support for all school districts.

49. Audit school bus routes by installing timers to measure the time needed to drive each distance.

50. Increase class size in Grades 3 through 5. (You can soften the impact by using teaching assistants to lower the adult-pupil ratio during reading and math periods.)

51. Cut out high-cost commencement speakers.

52. Monitor billing—especially telephone bills. (Experts estimate that 95% of business telephone bills contain mistakes—particularly billing for 800 numbers.)

53. Stretch the shelf life of reference materials by 1 year.

54. Increase the efficiency of e-mail usage.

E-mail Tips

- Establish a policy for e-mail use. Inform employees that e-mail is not a secure medium and that messages may be monitored. (An exception to the Federal Electronic Communications Privacy Act of 1986 permits employers to intercept messages deemed to be work related.)
- Limit the length of messages to a maximum of eight lines per paragraph.
- Use spaces instead of tabs for indenting.
- Stay away from fancy or elaborate fonts.
- Check all messages for grammar and spelling errors.
- Always use the subject line.
- Include a salutation and identify the intended receiver.
- Be concise—stick to the point.
- Cut down on attached documents.
- Avoid sending personal, sensitive, or confidential information.
- Don't send "flame mail" (e-mail messages sent in anger).
- Avoid sending unsolicited messages (junk mail, jokes, pyramid letters, etc.)
- Minimize use of emotions (e.g., smiley faces).
- Don't say anything via e-mail that you wouldn't say in person.
- Always let recipient know who else is getting the message.

55. Maintain good relations with union leaders and members. It can help minimize salary demands, reduce grievances, keep legal costs down, and increase productivity.

56. Speed up the construction of new facilities.

57. Shift overcrowded elementary pupils to vacant secondary schools and vice versa as needed.

58. Seek out undervalued property in your district and challenge its assessed valuation in hopes of obtaining added operating revenue.

59. Renovate existing facilities rather than constructing new buildings.

60. Renegotiate overgenerous benefits. (It's not easy. But if you've given away the farm, try to get some of it back over time.)

61. Keep track of what you own. Check warehouses and storage areas. You may find forgotten items such as pianos, desks, audio-visual equipment, and so on. If you discover forgotten inventory, sell it.

62. Hire your own media, computer, and office equipment repair personnel. It's often cheaper than paying outsiders to repair high-maintenance items.

63. Control door keys. (It cuts down on the overnight disappearance of materials and supplies.)

64. Schedule most cleaning personnel after school hours. Fewer people can do more faster when kids aren't around.

65. Consider starting smaller "charter schools" in existing public or private buildings rather than constructing a new large (and costly) high school.

66. Eliminate overnight athletic trips and limit meal allowances.

67. Adapt flexible work arrangements to get the most out of classified personnel.

68. Broaden professional roles and increase job flexibility in order to reduce the need for specialists.

69. Look for better ways to collect taxes. If your district has to collect its own taxes, you may be better off hiring a bank to do it for you.

70. Practice risk management to reduce the possibility of costly litigation. Carry adequate liability insurance. Listen to complaints and attempt to resolve disputes without going to court.

71. Save on insurance costs.

Insurance Tips

- Increase deductibles.
- Provide health-awareness education programs.
- Consider moving to self-insurance/managed care insurance.
- Pay stipends to staff members who don't use the district's health insurance plan.

---

72. Negotiate a provision for establishing a limited number of minimum wage "school keeper" (sweeper) positions to replace some higher-paid custodial positions.

73. Cut out expensive or elaborate end-of-year celebrations, such as grade-level theme park excursions.

74. Use standard notebook binders with computer-printed adhesive labels instead of special binders with embossed titles for curriculum guides, annual reports, and so forth.

75. Avoid costly contract buy-outs.

76. Capitalize on the hidden value of district-owned real estate assets by putting holding property to better use.

77. Consider using wind power (wind turbines) to generate electrical power. (It works for Spirit Lake, Iowa.)

78. Don't rent graduation caps and gowns for faculty, administration, and school board members at commencement time.

79. Look into buying battery-powered pick-up trucks for use by the building and grounds department within a 10-mile radius of your maintenance shop.

80. Eliminate duplication of expensive encyclopedias. (Who needs several different sets *and* computer encyclopedia software, too?)

81. Require administrators to teach a class and/or substitute occasionally.

82. Eliminate written reports no longer needed and simplify others by reducing the number of recipients, limiting attachments and appendices, and issuing them less often.

83. Lower teaching loads without increasing costs. Reduce the number of groups teachers teach by combining separate subject areas, lengthening the duration of classes, or having smaller groups work more intensely with teachers.

84. Check what's in the ground under school property. Mineral rights can be an unexpected source of income. Your district wouldn't be the first in the country to have an oil well on the school grounds.

85. If you need a new facility and want to save money, consider a lease-purchase arrangement whereby another party (the state, the school board association, etc.) builds the school and leases it to the district. After 30 to 40 years, ownership then reverts to the district.

86. Solicit ideas for more effective resource management. Offer incentives (VIP parking, limo service, etc.) for usable suggestions. Set aside one day a month to listen to employee and student complaints about perceived waste, extravagance, and inefficiencies.

87. Keep a bank of turned-down ideas. Some suggestions may be worth salvaging or recycling later on.

88. Do what smart business owners do. Examine all expenditures to identify items your school buys that you can readily live without.

Any school can find, save, or free up all the resources it needs. Most don't. It's not because they can't or don't want to. They simply don't get around to it.

The trick is to get started. Pick a strategy from the starter list above or identify one of your own and just do it. Then pick another for implementation. Then another. Once you've started, you'll learn new tricks every day.

Like physical conditioning, fiscal fitness gets easier as you go along. If you make efficiency a habit, soon you'll wonder how you ever got along without it.

Some teachers and administrators think that getting maximum value out of all the school's resources is easy. Just a matter of paying attention. It's not.

The time-honored economic principle, TINSTAFL (there is no such thing as free lunch), still applies. You can do more with less; but you can't do it with nothing. Worthy goals require workmanlike effort.

Resource management is a little like dieting. Although quick gains are possible, long-term success requires extraordinary focus, discipline, and perseverance. Not all educators possess these winning qualities. What about you?

Fiscal fitness is always hard work. It's always worthwhile, too. When people believe you're spending their money wisely, they're more willing to support the school in good times and bad.

8

Success Stories

All of the money-making and money-saving ideas outlined in the previous chapters sound great. But do they really work? Do real schools really do these things? You bet!

Every day of the year, countless schools and school districts in all parts of the nation are incorporating these measures and more. By using all they have and all they can get to full advantage, they are saving valuable resources without shortchanging any child's education.

Unfortunately, most of these schools don't brag about their successes (although they should). Fiscally fit schools are after results, not recognition. Acts of fiscal fitness are not glamorous or heroic. They are only necessary.

Most of the nation's schools that live within their means work their wonders without hoopla or fanfare. Occasionally, however, some of these success stories pop to the surface of public attention and recognition.

As early as 1996, School Match (a Columbus, Ohio-based research firm) identified for *American Demographics* journal the following nine districts as deserving of recognition for operating "low-spending, high-performance" schools:

1. Decatur (Alabama) City School District
2. Harrison (Arkansas) Public School District
3. Idaho Falls (Idaho) School District
4. Rock Island-Milan (Illinois) School District
5. Sierra Vista (Arizona) Unified School District
6. Solanco School District (Quarryville, Pennsylvania)
7. Valley Grove School District (Franklin, Pennsylvania)

8. Webster Groves (Missouri) School District (a suburb of St. Louis)

9. West Texas Independent School District

Although you may not have heard much about them, fiscal fitness is alive and well in these and a lot of other schools. Some are closer than you think.

Following are 10 more prime examples of schools and school districts that have been noticed for practicing the principles of fiscal fitness:

1. The Hanover (Virginia) Public School System is a past recipient of the prestigious U.S. Senate Award for Continuing Excellence in recognition of its efforts in applying business language and methods to help educate more students with fewer resources. Hanover is one of many schools that have made "productivity" a regular part of today's public school vocabulary.

2. Another award-winner is the Forest Grove (Oregon) District, which was honored with the 1996 Magna Award for its unique approach to involving staff and community members in setting priorities for budget reductions (see Chapter 3).

3. The Conestoga Valley District in Lancaster, Pennsylvania, has received attention for privatizing its food service division, allowing the schools to benefit from the profits.

The district has also established a nonprofit foundation that purchases stock and disperses educational grants to the schools out of the profits and dividends.

4. The Deer Park School District (Long Island, New York) has a proven track record of saving space, time, and expense by centralizing its high-volume printing and duplicating operations.

5. Enterprising entrepreneurship has helped the Gloucester (Massachusetts) School District balance its budget. To bring in additional revenue, the district assumed management of an indoor skating rink, operated concessions on city beaches, and started its own bus company. If your school is still stuck in the mode of candy and bake sales, you've got some catching up to do.

6. The Olathe (Kansas) Public Schools have earned the reputation as a leader in achieving significant cost savings through conservation of resources. For starters, the district contracted with an energy service company to replace outmoded lighting and controls and install weather stripping where needed. Olathe also participates in purchasing consortiums and co-ops to save money on everything from natural gas to school supplies.

7. Aquila Primary Center and Cedar Manor Intermediate Center in St. Louis Park, Minnesota, have received extensive publicity for initiating a model collaborative. The ACT program (Aquila-Cedar Manor Together) is a partnering effort between the schools and the Jewish Family and Children Services of Minneapolis, which provides one-stop social services for students and families.

With support from a variety of community agencies, Jewish Family and Children Services provides a team of mental health professionals (case manager, family support worker, social worker, prevention specialist, clinical therapist, psychologist, etc.) to help meet the emotional, social, and resource needs of at-risk children and families in the two schools. Services include the following:

- Weekly classroom self-esteem activities
- Assistance with conflict resolution
- Volunteer tutors and mentors
- Consultation with teachers
- In-house parenting education
- Parent support groups
- Referrals to mental health agencies
- Help with tapping community resources to find affordable housing, medical and dental care, access to food stamps, food, clothing, job training, and placement services

The schools contribute only in-kind services and the program is *free* to all families. You can't get a much better deal than that.

8. Historically, the New Haven (Connecticut) Schools have been known for using parents as resources to educate kids. Sometimes referred to as a "conspiracy of adults," the New Haven approach includes school management teams, paying one parent per classroom

a small stipend to serve as a teacher aide and involving parents in planning cocurricular activities.

9. The Montgomery County Schools in Rockford, Maryland, have also been featured in professional journals for successfully implementing a variety of efficiencies to save cost, including increasing intermediate class size with a minimum of opposition or resistance, entering into joint power agreements, and streamlining their food service programs.

10. In recent times, few schools have applied the principles of fiscal fitness better than St. Lukes High School in Jersey City, New Jersey. St. Lukes has gained nationwide attention as a poor (ghetto) parochial school that has turned scant resources into success through "rock hard" discipline, faith, and the untapped power of parents and teachers.

The school offers proof that it doesn't take deep pockets to have intense parental involvement and an effective discipline program. (The St. Luke's discipline plan features a no-nonsense detention component—"selective incarceration" where students are punished by being "forced" to listen to Frank Sinatra recordings.)

The depth and quality of the connection between home and school is exemplified by the fact that many teachers give out their home telephone numbers to selected students who are urged to call whenever they have a problem. With this kind of commitment and cooperation, schools don't need a blank check or unlimited resources to reach and teach today's young people.

So you see, there are real-world schools working out every day to achieve fiscal fitness. Of course, the best examples are those closest to home. You might be surprised by what some of your neighboring schools are doing to stretch resources and eliminate waste. They can help your school do the same. All you have to do is dare to ask. Your school could be the next big success story.

9

A Final Word

Fiscal fitness is the state of operating at peak efficiency and productivity. Isn't that the state you want your school to be in?

If you've read this far, you now know literally hundreds of ways to raise extra money, stretch resources, and even do more with less. But why would you ever do those things?

Not because you have to. Not because it will make you famous. Not because it's easy or fun. The only compelling reason for doing them is because it means a better education for kids.

Trying to find or save money or trying to make resources go further isn't a sign of weakness. It's a sign of strength and, more important, an indication of a commitment to get even stronger.

Holding the line on expenditures doesn't mean holding the line on learning. It simply means finally getting your priorities straight. It's making the most of whatever you have.

Believe it or not, your school is enough the way it is. Your school has or can get everything needed to reach its goals. For example, no matter how limited your assets, you still have the capability of initiating budget-neutral reforms. Likewise, even the most strapped school can use trade-offs to implement "enhancements." Any school is only as poor as its staff and leadership allow it to be.

Excellence is affordable for any school—including yours. It is within your grasp. Of course, you may have to reach. Stretch. Flex. Grunt. Sweat. It's not easy; it's only doable.

Reading this book can help. But reading won't get it done. Hard work will. The best time to start is now.

Some schools whine and wish for more. Others use what they have to get what they need. Some administrators make excuses. Others make things happen. It's a choice. What's yours?

Resource A

What Others Say About
Fiscal Fitness

*C*hildren are our most valuable resource.
—Herbert Hoover

≈

*T*he only limits are, as always, those of vision.
—James Broughton

≈

*C*hoice is always about giving up something.
—Dr. Laura Schlessinger

≈

*N*othing adds more power to your life than
concentrating on a limited set of targets.
—Nido Qubein

≈

*L*imited funds are a blessing, not a curse. Nothing encourages
creative thinking in quite the same way.
—H. Jackson Brown, Jr.

≈

*T*here are two ways to get enough: 1) accumulate
more and more; or 2) desire less.
—Anonymous

*E*conomy is a distributive virtue, and consists
not in saving but in selection.

—*Edmund Burke*

～

*T*he only means of conservation is innovation.

—*Peter Drucker*

～

*Y*ou can have anything you want, but you
can't have everything you want.

—*John Roger and Peter McWilliams*

～

*A*ppetite comes with eating; the more you eat,
the more you want.

—*Donna and Robert Leahy*

～

*W*here there's a will there's a way.

—*Proverb*

～

*W*e are wealthy and wasteful but this can't go on.

—*Magnus Pyke*

～

*A*re we willing to give up some things we like to do,
to move on to those things we must do?

—*Satenig St. Marie*

～

*O*ff the rack solutions, like bargain basement
dresses, never fit anyone.

—*Francoise Giroud*

*L*ess is more.

—*Robert Browning*

~

*D*on't ask for more. Ask for better.

—*Alan Cohen*

~

*N*ot everything that counts can be counted.

—*Anonymous*

~

*W*aste not, want not.

—*Proverb*

~

*E*conomy is the art of making the most of life.

—*George Bernard Shaw*

~

*N*othing in excess.

—*Anonymous*

~

*W*e are living beyond our means.

—*Margaret Mead*

~

*T*here is no such thing as free lunch.

—*Milton Friedman*

~

*B*ureaucracy defends the status quo long past
the time when the quo has lost its status.

—*Laurence J. Peter*

*B*eware of all enterprises that require new clothes.
—Henry David Thoreau

~

*M*ore is not always better. Sometimes, enough is better.
—Alan Cohen

~

*C*reate simplicity, not austerity.
—Elaine St. James

~

*L*ive beneath your means . . . Don't think a higher price always means higher quality.
—H. Jackson Brown, Jr.

~

I don't think you can spend yourself rich.
—George Humphrey

~

*L*ife is short and so is money.
—Bertolt Brecht

~

*L*ead with your values and make money too.
—Ben and Jerry

~

*E*nough is as good as a feast.
—John Heywood

~

*E*ven after a bad harvest there must be a sowing.
—Seneca

*T*here is enough for everyone's needs,
but not for everyone's greed.

—*Gandhi*

≈

*F*ocus on making things better, not bigger.

—*H. Jackson Brown, Jr.*

≈

*L*iving fully doesn't mean having it all.

—*Elaine St. James*

≈

*M*oney problems are really idea problems.

—*Dr. Robert Schuller*

≈

*W*hen there is something you want,
it seems it is everywhere.

—*Risa Mickenberg*

≈

*T*hese are the days when it takes all you've
got to keep up with the losers.

—*Robert Orben*

≈

*B*ills travel through the mail at twice the speed of checks.

—*Anonymous*

≈

*I*t is hard to pay for bread that has been eaten.

—*Danish Proverb*

*N*ever ask a lawyer or accountant for business advice.
They are trained to find problems, not solutions.

—*H. Jackson Brown, Jr.*

❧

*D*on't sweat the small stuff.

—*Richard Carlson*

❧

*E*ver tried? Ever failed? Try again. Fail again. Fail better.

—*Samuel Beckett*

❧

*T*here's a better way to do it . . . find it.

—*Thomas Edison*

❧

*A*s we say in the sewers, if you're not ready to go all
the way, don't put on your boots in the first place.

—*Ed Norton* (The Honeymooners)

Resource B

A Selected Bibliography for Today's Administrators

Brewer, E., & Achilles, C. (1998). *Finding funding.* Thousand Oaks, CA: Corwin.

Chernow, F., & Chernow, C. (1992). *Elementary principal's complete handbook.* Englewood Cliffs, NJ: Prentice Hall.

Epstein, J., Coates, L., Sanders, M. G., Simon, B. S., & Salinas, K. C. (1998). *School, family, and community partnerships.* Thousand Oaks, CA: Sage.

Ramsey, R. (1992). *Secondary principal's survival guide.* Englewood Cliffs, NJ: Prentice Hall.

Ramsey, R. (1999). *Lead, follow, or get out of the way.* Thousand Oaks, CA: Corwin.

Ruskin, K., & Achilles, C. (1995). *Grantwriting, fundraising, and partnerships.* Thousand Oaks, CA: Corwin.

St. James, E. (1995). *Simplify your life.* New York: Hyperion.

Warner, C. (2000). *Promoting your school* (2nd edition). Thousand Oaks, CA: Corwin.

CORWIN
PRESS

The Corwin Press logo—a raven striding across an open book—represents the happy union of courage and learning. We are a professional-level publisher of books and journals for K–12 educators, and we are committed to creating and providing resources that embody these qualities. Corwin's motto is "Success for All Learners."